PRAISE FOR
THE APOSTLES' CREED

"I make it a habit to read everything that Albert Mohler writes. Even when I already know and embrace the truths that he is teaching in his writings, the way he looks at topics, explains them, and even his turns of phrases help me better communicate and appreciate those same truths. Every Christian will profit from this book. No one has labored with greater earnestness or cost to defend Christian truth in our own time than Albert Mohler. You can count on this presentation of central Christian doctrine to be faithful to God's Word, from a heart that burns with Gospel commitment to God's truth."

—J. Ligon Duncan, chancellor and CEO,
Reformed Theological Seminary

"Many Christians outside the more liturgical traditions never recite the Apostles' Creed. Dr Mohler wants to change that. As he points out, Christians may believe more than what is asserted in the creed, but it is impossible to be a Christian while believing less. The Apostles' Creed not only summarizes a great deal of common Christian belief, but it fosters individual and corporate recitation—and by regular recitation of the creed with other Christians, believers join the assembly of believers across the ages, even while they give substance to their faith with the opening words of deepest confession: 'I believe. . . .' In twenty crisp chapters, Dr. Mohler summarizes the theology carried along by each phrase or clause of the creed, a kind of A-B-C of fundamental Christian belief."

—D. A. Carson, professor of the New Testament
and founder of the Gospel Coalition

"Albert Mohler, one of the outstanding theologians of this generation, has provided a thoughtful, insightful, and biblically informed commentary on the Apostles' Creed. Offering a clearly written and incisive introduction to this important confessional statement, this volume clarifies for readers the meaning of the essential truths of the Christian faith. Pastors, Christian leaders, and students will all be grateful for this engaging, convictional, and astute work."

—David S. Dockery, president, Trinity International University, Trinity Evangelical Divinity School

"This is an essential book for those who want to see an ancient creed infuse new life into a decaying generation. Dr. Mohler brings to this project not only his impressive theological knowledge of our ancient faith, but also a keen awareness of the new questions our culture poses to it. He expounds with clarity and simplicity the faith delivered once for all to the saints, showing that it still possesses the power to turn the world upside down."

—J. D. Greear, pastor, The Summit Church; president, Southern Baptist Convention

THE APOSTLES' CREED

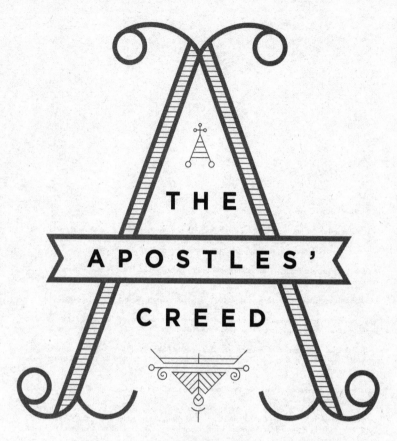

THE APOSTLES' CREED

DISCOVERING AUTHENTIC CHRISTIANITY IN AN AGE OF COUNTERFEITS

R. ALBERT MOHLER JR.

NELSON
BOOKS

An Imprint of Thomas Nelson

Published in Nashville, Tennessee, by Nelson Books, an imprint of Thomas Nelson. Nelson Books and Thomas Nelson are registered trademarks of HarperCollins Christian Publishing, Inc.

Published in association with the literary agency of Wolgemuth & Associates, Inc.

Thomas Nelson titles may be purchased in bulk for educational, business, fund-raising, or sales promotional use. For information, please e-mail SpecialMarkets@ThomasNelson.com.

Unless otherwise noted, Scripture quotations are taken from the ESV® Bible (The Holy Bible, English Standard Version®). Copyright © 2001 by Crossway, a publishing ministry of Good News Publishers. Used by permission. All rights reserved.

Scripture quotations marked CEV are from the Contemporary English Version. Copyright © 1991, 1992, 1995 by American Bible Society. Used by permission.

Scripture quotations marked HCSB are from the Holman Christian Standard Bible®. Copyright © 1999, 2000, 2002, 2003, 2009 by Holman Bible Publishers. Used by permission. HCSB® is a federally registered trademark of Holman Bible Publishers.

Scripture quotations marked KJV are from the King James Version. Public domain.

Scripture quotations marked NIV are from the Holy Bible, New International Version®, NIV®. Copyright © 1973, 1978, 1984, 2011 by Biblica, Inc.® Used by permission of Zondervan. All rights reserved worldwide. www.Zondervan.com. The "NIV" and "New International Version" are trademarks registered in the United States Patent and Trademark Office by Biblica, Inc.®

Italics in Scripture have been added by the author for emphasis.

Any Internet addresses, phone numbers, or company or product information printed in this book are offered as a resource and are not intended in any way to be or to imply an endorsement by Thomas Nelson, nor does Thomas Nelson vouch for the existence, content, or services of these sites, phone numbers, companies, or products beyond the life of this book.

ISBN 978-1-4002-1480-8 (TP)
ISBN 978-0-7180-9918-3 (eBook)
ISBN 978-0-7180-9915-2 (HC)

Library of Congress Control Number: 2018961099

Printed in the United States of America

20 21 22 23 24 LSC 10 9 8 7 6 5 4 3 2 1

Dedicated to
Henry Albert Barnes

Grandson of priceless gratitude, source of incredible joy, promise of the future, sign of divine love. You bear the names of kings, a sign of great expectation. You bear a name we share, a sign of the faithfulness of God from generation to generation. You are so loved by your parents, your grandparents, and your big brother, Benjamin. Just even to think of you makes us unspeakably happy. May you know even a taste of the joy you have brought to us, and above all, may you come to know Christ, so that one glorious day you will say, in the faith of the apostles and the communion of Christ's saints throughout the ages, "I believe."

Papa

CONTENTS

CONTENTS

I believe in God, the Father Almighty,
Maker of heaven and earth,
and in Jesus Christ, his only Son, our Lord;
Who was conceived of the Holy Spirit,
born of the Virgin Mary,
suffered under Pontius Pilate,
was crucified, dead, and buried.
He descended into hell.
The third day he arose again from the dead.
He ascended into heaven
and sits at the right hand of God the Father Almighty,
whence he shall come to judge the quick and the dead.
I believe in the Holy Spirit,
the holy catholic Church,
the communion of saints,
the forgiveness of sins,
the resurrection of the body,
and the life everlasting.
Amen.

FOREWORD

It struck me that Dr. Mohler's statement in the introduction: "All Christians believe more than is contained in the Apostles' Creed, but none can believe less," is crucial to the very purpose of his book. This classic summary of Christian belief first appeared in the fourth century and has been memorized, recited, and included in the worship of Christians since then.

Many declare that it is all that anyone needs to believe to be counted among the true believers and therefore it is the basis of Christian unity. For them it is the "mere Christianity" that unites us all. Some have stated that the true nonnegotiables are all settled by the Apostles' Creed so that anyone who gives assent to that ancient creed should be embraced as a true Christian.

In reality, the creed leaves out essential doctrines like the authority of Scripture, the depravity of man, the deity of Christ, and the means of salvation: justification by faith. It also contains nonessentials like the role of Pilate and the descent to hell.

In 1681 a godly Dutch reformed theologian named Herman Witsius published, in Latin, a series of dissertations on the

Apostles' Creed (recently republished). He did this to put the theological meat on the bones of this beautiful statement. It was in the 1800s that William Cunningham (one of the founders of the Free Church of Scotland and the author of *Historical Theology*) wrote regarding the creed, "If men appeal to the creed as proof of their orthodoxy they are, of course, bound to explain its meaning."

It is time for this generation to be given the same gift that those men gave past generations. Dr. Mohler has done that. Here it is in fresh, doctrinally rich insights from our trusted friend and biblical scholar, who with the bright light of his sanctified mind illuminates the riches outlined in these ancient words. Read and see.

John MacArthur

INTRODUCTION

I believe; help my unbelief!

—MARK 9:24

It began as an assignment. It ended as a milestone in my Christian life. My church history professor assigned the class to memorize the Apostles' Creed. Obediently, I began to memorize this historic affirmation of the Christian faith word by word, phrase by phrase, truth by truth. Within a few hours I had committed the Apostles' Creed to memory, ready when called upon in class to recite it. But even at that time I knew that something else had happened.

As a young man I realized that this ancient confession of faith is Christianity. This is what Christians believe—what all Christians believe. The Apostles' Creed collapses time and space, uniting all true believers in the one, holy, and apostolic faith. This creed is a summary of what the Bible teaches, a narrative of God's redemptive love, and a concise statement of basic Christianity.

All Christians believe more than is contained in the Apostles' Creed, but none can believe less.

Ancient Christians honored this creed. Martyrs recited this creed. The Protestant Reformers continued the use of the Apostles' Creed in worship and the teaching of believers.

There is such power in knowing that when we confess the Apostles' Creed, alone or in corporate worship, we are declaring the truth of the Christian faith with the very words that gave early Christians hope, sent martyrs confidently to their deaths, and have instructed Christ's church throughout the centuries.

It was the most important class assignment I ever had.

I believe. These two words are among the most explosive words any human can utter. They open the door to eternal life and are the foundation of the Christian faith. Belief stands as the very center of Christian faithfulness and is where Christianity begins for the Christian. We enter the faith and find eternal life in Christ by responding to the truth with trust—that is, with belief.

But Christianity is not belief in *belief*. It is belief in a propositional truth: that Jesus is the Christ, the Son of God, and savior of sinners. We do not believe in a Christ of our imagination but in the Christ of Scripture—the Christ believed in by every generation of true Christians. Furthermore, beyond belief in Christ stands belief in everything Jesus taught his disciples. Matthew recorded that Jesus instructed his disciples to teach others to observe all that he had commanded them (Matt. 28:18–20). Therefore, there is no Christianity without belief, without teaching, and without obedience to Christ.

But where do we turn in order to know how to believe and what to believe? We turn first, of course, to the Bible, the very Word of God. The Bible is our only sufficient source and unerring rule of faith, and the Christian reflex to turn to the Bible is always right. The Bible is without error, totally trustworthy, and true. It is the verbally inspired Word of God. Nothing can be added to it or taken from it. When we read the New Testament, we find the faith handed down from Christ to the apostles, those who were taught by Christ himself. Any form of belief that does not agree with the teaching of Christ to the apostles is false—a religion that cannot save.

The New Testament refers to authentic Christianity as "the faith that was once for all delivered to the saints" (Jude 3). Real Christianity is Christianity resting on truth—a faith of definite beliefs cherished by believers throughout the ages and *once for all* given to the church.

This is one of the great wonders of Christianity and explains why all true Christians hold to the same essential beliefs and have done so for two thousand years: as Christians, we believe what the apostles believed. And we want to hand that same faith to the next generation.

Further, we want to worship like the apostles and preach and teach like them. To do so, we turn first to the Bible, but we also turn to the historic and faithful summaries of the Christian faith, the most honored, historic, and universal of which is the Apostles' Creed.

From its earliest beginnings the church has faced the dual challenge of affirming the truth and confronting error. Over the centuries, the church has turned to a series of creeds and confessions of faith in order to define and defend true Christianity. The confession of faith we know as the Apostles' Creed is one of the most important of these confessions. For long, unbroken centuries it has stood as one of the most crucial teaching instruments of the Christian faith—along with the Ten Commandments and the Lord's Prayer.

The Apostles' Creed was not written by the apostles, but it does reflect the early church's effort to express and summarize the faith given by Christ to the apostles. Early Christians called the creed "the rule of faith" and turned to it as they worshipped and taught the faithful. But the question arises: Why today, do we need a book on the Apostles' Creed? What relevance could it have and what benefit can come from examining it? Some object to the very idea of accountability to old words. Still others claim that Christians are to hold no creed but the Bible and to have "no creed but Christ." The problem is, of course, that we all need a summary of what the Bible teaches, and the church needs a strong standard for recognizing true Christianity and rejecting false doctrines.

What is more, behind some objections to the Apostles' Creed is something exceedingly dangerous: a desire for a doctrineless faith. Some argue for a Christianity that requires no formal doctrines or doctrinal mandates. The history of Christianity, however, is littered with the debris of many such movements, each of which left behind shattered lives of people whose faith dissolved without the structure of doctrine.

The idea of a doctrineless Christianity stands at odds with the words of Christ, who revealed himself to the apostles in explicitly doctrinal terms. Jesus revealed himself in truth claims. He identified himself as the Son of Man and demonstrated his deity, even referring to himself as "I am" repeatedly in the gospel of John—bearing the name God had given himself from the burning bush as he spoke to Moses (Ex. 3:13–16). A doctrineless Christianity also stands in contradiction with what Christ commissioned his apostles to do—to make disciples of all nations and to teach them to obey all that Christ commanded (Matt. 28:18–20). This command requires doctrine.

Here we have to remember simply that doctrine, as a great historian of Christianity explained it, is "what the church believes, teaches, and confesses on the basis of the word of God."[1] Any church that believes, teaches, and worships has some doctrine. The question is: Are they the right doctrines, the right teachings?

The Apostles' Creed stands as a timeless distillation of the Christian faith. The creed instructs, guides, defends, and enshrines the glorious truths that answer the most important question anyone could ask: "What must I do to be saved?" The Philippian jailor asked that same question of Paul, and Paul responded, *"Believe* in the Lord Jesus" (Acts 16:30–31).

This response reveals, once again, the absolute centrality of belief to the Christian faith. And this belief has an object: Jesus Christ. The Scriptures, however, contain fundamental truths that believers must also cherish and affirm. Creeds serve that pursuit of truth that is necessary for faithful Christian witness. For almost two thousand years, the Apostles' Creed has provided the church with a venerable summary of core Christian doctrine. It distinguishes truth from error, light from darkness, and life from death. Indeed, the Apostles' Creed stands as a landmark of orthodoxy to guide the church.

Each stanza of the Apostles' Creed begins with the Latin word *credo*, "I believe." Like Paul's response to the Philippian jailor, the creed affirms the integral connection of faith to the Christian life. Christians are a believing people, and they place their belief in the objective truth claims of the Scriptures. Truth, therefore, does not rest in subjective feelings of right and wrong. Truth flows from the objective reality of the blood of Jesus Christ, where God revealed his glory, his will, and his purpose for all mankind. Truth comes from what God has done for sinners in Christ. As the church recognized this truth, it sought to enshrine it in creeds or affirmations of what Christians believe to be true, essential, and splendid—splendid because they allow the splendor of truth and the splendor of Christ to be fully seen.

A study on the Apostles' Creed, therefore, could not be more relevant in this age of modernity. A cultural revolution has swept across the West, blurring the lines between reality and fiction. Entire Christian denominations have capitulated to the whims of this revolution and surrendered the fundamental truths of their faith. In this surrender these churches have lost their identity as God's people. All churches, therefore, must recapture and reinvigorate their zeal for all the doctrines contained in the Apostles' Creed. Each and every *credo* encapsulates the very essence and foundation of what the people of God believe—and what they have *always* believed.

In light of this reality, Christians must stand firm and stand together on the essential truths of Scripture. The church fathers understood this fact, which is why they labored so diligently to give the church faithful summaries of Scripture's teaching, like the Apostles' Creed.

As we examine the creed, consider these seven reasons why the Apostles' Creed is useful and necessary in the life of the church.

1. *Creeds define the truth.* Jesus Christ told his disciples, "And you will know the truth, and the truth will set you free" (John 8:32). We must study the creeds of the faith, so long as they rightly espouse the Scriptures, because they outline the truths of our faith. The truth sets the people of God free from sin, corruption, and a world under the despair of sin. The truth ushers in an eternal hope in the

glorious splendor of God and his gospel to mankind. As the creeds teach the truth, they espouse a power that sets the captive free.

2. *Creeds correct error.* The reality of truth presupposes the existence of error. In the present age, however, we find a generation, perhaps for the first time, that objects to the existence of truth. The church, however, has understood since its founding that heresy and false teaching exist and that these are horrible dangers to the people of God. Indeed, no error presents a greater danger to the church and the world than theological error. Heresy, the denial of a doctrine central to Christianity, departs from the truth and thus has eternal consequences. The church needs the creeds not only to teach the truth but to guard against error.

3. *Creeds provide rules and standards for God's people.* The Apostles' Creed functions as a guardrail for our teaching and instruction. Indeed, the creeds protect teachers from stumbling into error by providing a rule to follow and boundaries for healthy theological discussion and development. One of the most important functions of the Apostles' Creed, like all faithful creeds, is that it helps the church to teach and prepare new believers for faithfulness and maturity in the faith of the church. New believers in the early church were often asked to affirm the lines of the Apostles' Creed, one by one affirming their belief and confession of the true Christian faith.

4. *Creeds teach the church how to worship and confess the faith.* The Apostles' Creed delineates the most glorious and splendid truths of the Christian faith. It naturally ushers our souls into heartfelt worship and praise of God.

The creeds, therefore, guide the church in worship and contain the most precious truths through which we can worship God and rightly praise his name. In corporate worship, voices converge so that *I believe* becomes *we believe*, joining together all believers, both the living and those already with Christ.

5. *Creeds connect us to the faith of our fathers.* The late historical theologian Jaroslav Pelikan wrote, "Tradition is the living faith of the dead, traditionalism is the dead faith of the living."[2] Indeed, the annals of church history and the venerable creeds of the faith contain some of the most precious inheritances modern Christians possess. The Apostles' Creed, more than words on a page, contains the faithful witness of those who have finished the race faithfully. We have a blood-bought relationship with our brothers and sisters who went before us. We joyfully desire to stand in the same faith with them—all the way back to the apostles.

6. *Creeds summarize the faith.* No creed or statement of faith can replace the Scriptures. As we have seen, however, this does not mean that creeds have no place in the Christian life. Those who would argue for no creed but the Bible have forfeited a great gift in maintaining biblical Christianity. This dubious position fails to understand the heart behind creeds and confessions. These documents do not seek to *replace* Scripture. Instead, they accurately seek to summarize its content into succinct statements in order to equip Christians with brief yet crucial distillations of the faith.

7. *Creeds define true Christian unity.* Finally, the affirmations of the Apostles' Creed weave a fabric that knits

all Christians together in the genuine bonds of unity. Statements of faith and the creeds of the church unite believers from all ages to the unchanging truth of God's revelation. Indeed, the affirmations of these creeds can bridge denominational divides as brothers and sisters from across the globe and throughout all history gather together around the pillars of the faith, the essence of what it means to be Christian. True Christian unity is unity in the truth revealed by Christ, not unity at the expense of truth, as is becoming all too common. The Apostles' Creed does not confess some lowest-common-denominator form of Christian truth. It boldly confesses the grandeur of authentic Christianity in a series of powerful statements of Christian belief.

Now we see why a study of the Apostles' Creed is not merely interesting but urgently needed. The Apostles' Creed, this most venerable of creeds, exposits the fundamental core of the Christian faith. It contains within its affirmations spectacular and eternal truths. Indeed, wrapped up in the Apostles' Creed is nothing less than the unfathomable riches of our God, the surpassing knowledge of Christ, and the true theological identity of Christ's people. That is why we will consider each phrase of the creed, one by one, in order to mine its riches, chapter by chapter.

CHAPTER ONE

GOD, THE FATHER ALMIGHTY

How do we even begin to speak of God, and by what right can we call him our Father? The audacity of claiming to speak of God seems massive enough, but then we go on to dare to call the almighty God our Father? This is exactly what Christians do and are taught by Jesus to do. Jesus taught his disciples to pray, "*Our Father* who is in heaven" (Matt. 6:9 NASB).

Modern theologians have had a big problem with the God of the Bible. When I was a freshly minted seminary student, I was assigned a book by Harvard University theologian Gordon Kaufman entitled *God the Problem*.[1] Kaufman wrote his book just a few years after *Time* magazine had scandalized the nation with its cover story from April 8, 1966, "Is God Dead?" The cover story reported that many academic theologians and liberal professors no longer believed in God. Kaufman argued that modern theologians needed to invent an entirely new language for speaking about God. The language found in the Bible, he believed, was out-of-date and unworthy of modern thinkers.

Kaufman went on to argue that theologians must find a new way to argue that the word *God* is still meaningful. The God who existed in older theology no longer exists, and so existing theologians, he argued, must find a new way of speaking of God as real. But Kaufman was uncomfortable with speaking of God as real in any sense. His book was, in the end, a kind of argument for employing theologians at schools like Harvard University when their theologians no longer believed in God.

A few days into class, an anonymous student drew a satirical cartoon on the class chalkboard of a book entitled *Gordon Kaufman the Problem* by God. The whole class got the point immediately. If there is a theological problem, it is not God. The problem is us.

Contrary to Kaufman and the "God is dead" theologians, we do know how to speak about God, and we do know who God is. The reason we know these things is because God has spoken. God has revealed himself in both nature and Scripture, and what separates modern theology from biblical Christianity is the modern lack of respect for Scripture and for the authority of God. Instead of relying on God's self-revelation in Scripture, so many modern theologies choose speculation and conjecture as their theological method. Much of this filters down into a form of postmodern pop spirituality, which has little to do with historic Christianity and biblical teaching.

Pop spirituality pervades self-help conferences, bestselling books, and television talk shows. These fools speak about the "supernatural," the "sacred," the "numinous," the "holy," the "divine," the "unconditional," or the "ground of being." But no vague, nondescript, ambiguous deity can save—only *God* can save. These evasive and generalized idols of God amount to little more than flimsy little idolatries. None of these can substitute for the self-revelation of God in the Bible. What Christians desperately need at this time is to return to historic Christianity, the Christianity that emerged from the rich doctrinal commitments and evangelistic fervor of the apostles.

Our Self-Revealing God

A. W. Tozer brilliantly summarized the entirety of Christian discipleship when he said, "What comes into our minds when we think of God is the most important thing about us."[2] What the church means when it says the word *God* reveals everything about our worship and theological integrity. If we begin with a wrong conception of God, we will misconstrue the entirety of the Christian faith. This fact is why heretics and false teachers so often begin by rejecting the doctrine of the Trinity. If we can reject God as he has revealed himself in Scripture, then we can and will reject everything else.

From the time of the apostles onward, the church has taken its stand on the phrase, *Credo in Deum Patrem Omnipotentem*: I believe in God, the Father Almighty. Notice, the Apostles' Creed does not begin merely with the words: "I believe in God." Rather, it goes beyond that simple phrase to describe the identity and character of God. The Christian faith is not established on some abstract deity or on "some god." We do not confess, "I believe in the numinous. We are here in the name of the supernatural, the sacred, and the divine." We do not call ourselves together in the name of the "thrice unconditioned," or some other form of speculation.

According to Scripture, everyone knows that God exists even if they claim to reject that knowledge. As Paul wrote, God's "invisible attributes, namely, his eternal power and divine nature," are "clearly perceived" (Rom. 1:20). The problem is that humanity rejects that revelation and suppresses the truth in unrighteousness (Rom. 1:18). The consequences of this truth suppression are abysmal confusion, fatal and futile speculation. Instead of turning to the God who has revealed himself in creation, men make idols for themselves or deny God's very existence—a conviction the Bible condemns as complete foolishness (Ps. 14:1).

Without God's revelation of himself, we would be utterly lost. We are not sufficiently intelligent, clever, or perceptive enough to come to a true knowledge of the true God on our own. This fact is why God's revelation of himself is so gracious. As evangelical theologian Carl F. H. Henry so beautifully explained, God loves us so much that "He forfeits His own personal privacy that His creatures might know Him."[3] If God had not denied himself his personal privacy, if he had not revealed himself to us, then we would be lost and locked in the same patterns of speculation, confusion, and futility that affects those who have not believed the Holy Scriptures. Only Scripture clearly exposes who God is and who we are.

Our hearts are corrupted to such a degree that we are ignorant without God's self-revelation. Calvin described the human heart in its fallen state as a "perpetual factory of idols,"[4] constantly producing and processing new idols of the imagination. Sometimes these idols take material form, but in our day, idols usually take philosophical and ideological forms.

This fact was demonstrated several decades ago when sociologists in Great Britain conducted a massive study on the religious convictions of British people—specifically of their belief in God.[5] What the survey revealed is that even many who believe in a god do not believe that he is personal, intervenes in human history, or has anything to do with the person and work of Christ. One responder to the survey summarized this view of god quite succinctly. When asked, "How would you describe the god in whom you believe?" he said, "Oh, just an ordinary god."

Many people we interact with in our neighborhoods and work places believe only in an "ordinary god." Far more hauntingly, even many people who sit next to us in worship believe in "just an ordinary god." This ordinary god is not the God of the Bible. Our concern with the first article of the creed is not with just an ordinary god or with the god of the philosophers but with the holy God who has revealed himself in Scripture.

The Christian identity is marked by the confession of God, the Father Almighty. The content of the Christian faith begins with the affirmation of the God who is, who spoke, and who revealed himself. When the Apostles' Creed begins with these words: "I believe in God, the Father Almighty," it immediately gets to the essential content of our faith—God's Trinitarian nature. Without this affirmation Christianity is incoherent—it does not hold together.

Our Father: A Personal God

The creed, like Scripture, indicates that the first person of the Trinity has revealed himself to us as "Father." In other words, this is not some distant, unknowable deity but a God with whom we have a personal relationship. God is not a force or a principle or a "higher power." He has instead revealed himself as the Father of our Lord Jesus Christ (Eph. 1:3).

The revelation of God as "Father" has roots in the Old Testament, where God is described as the Father of Israel (Deut. 32:6). The fatherly love of God is also present throughout the Old Testament. The prophet Hosea spoke of God as a Father carrying Israel as a child (Hos. 11:1–4), and David described God as a "Father of the fatherless" (Ps. 68:5).

The complete revelation of God as Father comes with the life and ministry of Jesus. Jesus, as "the Son," had a unique relationship with the Father. On one occasion, Jesus said, "I and the Father are one" (John 10:30). Another time he asserted, "I have come down from heaven, not to do my own will but the will of him who sent me" (John 6:38). The union between the Father and the Son transcends human associations and is part of the mystery of the Trinity—that God is one, and that the Father, the Son, and the Holy Spirit are God.

If properly understood, this Trinitarian relationship—unity in Trinity and Trinity in unity—will inspire and teach us how to relate to the God of Scripture, who is both personal and transcendent. In fact, Jesus was the one who taught us that we could call God "our Father" when he instructed his disciples to pray with these words: "Our Father in heaven, hallowed be your name" (Matt. 6:9). These words imply that Jesus' disciples are not only allowed to pray to God, but we are specifically instructed to pray to God as "Father."

Understanding the Trinitarian relationship and the role of the Father is not just a matter of theory but a central pillar in the life of every Christian. As Helmut Thielicke reminded us, the parable of the prodigal son is perhaps better understood as the "Parable of the Waiting Father,"[6] because in this passage we see a picture of God's personal, saving, and lavish care for those who repent and turn to him. By union with Christ the true Son, we also become sons of God. And as Paul reminded us, if we are sons then we are also heirs of the kingdom of God (Gal. 4:7).

Regrettably, many theologians have used the doctrine of the fatherhood of God to misrepresent his character and promote heretical teaching regarding both God and his redemptive work. Nineteenth-century liberals were particularly guilty of this error, arguing that God's fatherly love could be claimed by anyone, even those outside of Christ. As many historians have noted, many nineteenth-century liberals had only two principal doctrines: "The Fatherhood of God, the Brotherhood of Man."

In one sense we must indeed affirm that God is "fatherly" toward all his creation and exercises a providential care over all humanity. The fact that any human being anywhere exists and lives and breathes is a testimony to a paternal and benevolent relationship between the Creator and his creation. But this does not mean that God is "Father" in a personal and saving way to everybody. Scripture clearly affirms that we become sons of God only as we are united to Christ and thereby adopted into God's family (Gal. 4:4–5; Eph. 1:4–5).

The Baptist Faith and Message summarizes these points helpfully when it affirms:

God as Father reigns with providential care over His universe, His creatures, and the flow of the stream of human history according to the purposes of His grace. He is all powerful, all knowing, all loving, and all wise. God is Father in truth to those who become children of God through faith in Jesus Christ. He is fatherly in His attitude toward all men.

7

The fact that humans have a world to live in along with the gift of food and natural resources is evidence that God sustains humanity as in a fatherly way. Without God's daily provision all life would rapidly perish. For, "in him we live and move and have our being" (Acts 17:28). Life itself is a gift.

At the same time, recognizing God as the source and sustainer of humanity does not entail any form of universalism. It is one thing to assert that the Father "makes his sun rise on the evil and on the good, and sends rain on the just and on the unjust" (Matt. 5:45). It is quite another to affirm that God is obligated to save all because he is Father. In the Bible the path to truly knowing God as Father in a saving sense is through the Son, and only through the Son. As Jesus said, "Whoever has seen me has seen the Father" (John 14:9), for "I and the Father are one" (John 10:30). Only through the Son do we come to know the Father.

God, Our Mother?

Besides universalism, some theologians have also attacked the notion of God as Father on another front. Feminist theologians, for example, reject naming God as Father. Feminists see the title "Father" as evidence of ancient and repressive patriarchalism. Mary Daly most famously said, "If God is male, then the male is God."[7] That statement, however, is problematic at virtually every level. To say that God is Father is not to say that God has a gender. We simply speak as the Bible speaks. We affirm God is Father, Son, and Spirit. That affirmation does not imply that God has a gender in the same way as his human creatures. As Carl Henry stated:

The God of the Bible is a sexless God. When Scripture speaks of God as "he" the pronoun is primarily personal (generic) rather than masculine (specific); it emphasizes God's personality—and, in turn, that of the Father, Son and Spirit as Trinitarian distinctions—in contrast to impersonal entities.[8]

This masculine language is not only written within the warp and woof of Scripture. It is necessary to the understanding of the reality of the Trinity: the Father, Son, and Holy Spirit. To tamper with this is not merely to be creative in worship; it is to create a false god. We have no right to petition for a change.

Yet, in the last forty years, certain theologians and Bible translators have demanded that we change Scripture's "masculine" language about God. In that time several denominations have issued new hymn books and liturgies brimming with revisionist and feminist reimaginings of God's identity. In 2006 the Presbyterian Church USA adopted a report that allowed members of the denomination to experiment with new Trinitarian titles—titles they asserted would not replace Father, Son, and Holy Spirit but would instead supplement them.[9]

The report suggests that in addition to the traditional Trinitarian formula we could now speak in triads such as "Rainbow, Arch, and Dove,"[10] "Rock, Cornerstone, and Temple,"[11] and even "Fire that Consumes, Sword that Divides, and Storm that Melts Mountains."[12] The most explicitly feminist of these formulas was: "Compassionate Mother, Beloved Child, Life-giving Womb."[13] That "trinity," as well as the others, is decidedly not the God of the Bible; it is an idol.

Additionally, others have objected to calling God "Father" because they believe that for many people this term evokes abusive or absent fathers. In light of that sad fact, they argue, this term should be jettisoned. Although it is truly a tragedy that many children have grown up without invested, loving, grace-filled fathers, this fact does not grant us the right to assume that our own negative perceptions of fathers can be mapped onto the fatherhood of God. Rather, we are to see God's self-disclosure of his own character and his own being in Scripture as the ideal fatherhood. It is God the Father who defines what a human father must be like, not the other way around. The very fact that we know what human fathers *ought* to be like demonstrates that we know an ideal father does indeed exist. As a result, we will never recover family life and a true understanding of fatherhood until we can affirm without hesitation or mental reservation, "I believe in God, the Father Almighty."

The Father Almighty

The Apostles' Creed does not merely affirm, "I believe in God the Father," but it adds, "I believe in God, the Father *Almighty*." Just as God is personal, he is also all-powerful. God is imma-nent, but he is also transcendent. As Scripture indicates, God is *El Shaddai*, the God who is all-powerful (Gen. 17:1 CEV). This affirmation of God's absolute sovereignty drives all that follows in the creed. God is the one who is all-powerful, all-knowing, and ruling creation. Even king Nebuchadnezzar confessed, "He does according to his will among the host of heaven and among the inhabitants of the earth; and none can stay his hand or say to him, 'What have you done?'" (Dan. 4:35).

In the Apostles' Creed the word *Almighty* is a collective that is meant to represent all God's attributes, the fullness of God's perfections. All God's attributes—omnipotence, omniscience, omnipresence, self-existence, and immutability—are summed up in this one word, *Almighty*. Only the God who possesses the fullness of perfection and infinite majesty can truly be almighty and sovereign over creation.

Regrettably, the "God, the Father Almighty" affirmed in the creed is rarely discussed in many churches. Shallow descriptions of God and sloganeering are substituted for Christianity's rich confessional heritage. Regrettably, many pulpits proclaim a truncated and distorted vision of God. Many preachers fail to open up Scripture's rich teaching on God's holiness, righteousness, glory, and majesty and merely proclaim "just an ordinary god." The God of Christianity is not just an ordinary god. He is the Father Almighty; the Father who can do anything; the Father who possesses all power, the one who created by the power of his word and who rules forever.

Worshipping the Father Almighty

The creed starts with an affirmation that God is the Father Almighty. This truth is also where our worship begins. As Peter Martyr Vermigli, a lesser-known leader of the Reformation, said, this one statement of the creed should "dismiss as nonsense whatever troublesome men or your own disturbing thoughts suggest in contradiction to what the sacred oracles or divine promises contain."[14] We measure every doctrine and every thought against this affirmation about God's sovereign authority. If it falls short, we should, as Vermigli asserted, dismiss it as "nonsense."

God the Father Almighty is the God we worship in song, deeds, and in the preaching of God's Word. All hymns must reflect and resound to this glorious King. All preaching must fit his glorious reign. All works of service and love must be rendered for the glory of his name. This affirmation of God as "Father Almighty" ought to rule our hymnody, our teaching, and every moment of our daily lives.

CHAPTER TWO

MAKER OF HEAVEN AND EARTH

Why does the universe exist? How do we explain the cosmos—right down to our own individual existence? These are questions no intelligent person can avoid, and the answers to these questions determine just about every meaningful question that will follow.

In our age many believe that the cosmos is only an accident, utterly without design or a designer. The entire universe is just a natural fact with no transcendent meaning. And, if this is true of the entire universe, it is also true of you and of me.

Christians believe that everything that exists traces its existence and its reality to the sovereign act of God the Father Almighty—maker of heaven and earth. God, the maker of heaven and earth, is both Creator and Sustainer of all that is, all that ever was, and all that ever will be.

The creed begins with telling us who God is as the Father Almighty and what he has done as Maker of heaven and earth. Scripture also begins with God as Creator, "In the beginning, God created the heavens and the earth" (Gen. 1:1). Right from the start, Genesis 1:1 establishes some central and essential truths about God. First, God is eternal, existing prior to creation. Second, God is infinite, not bound by the heavens and the earth. Third, God is omnipotent, speaking creation into existence. Finally, God is independent, not relying on anything in creation. These truths are taught in those first four words of Scripture, "In the beginning, God." If we truly grasp this opening phrase of Scripture, the rest of our theological conviction will fall rightly into place. If we fail to truly understand these opening words, we may find ourselves on the quick road to idolatry.

Worldview Clash

The most fundamental features of our worldview are rooted in our doctrine of creation. Every worldview has a theory of origins, and how we understand our origins will influence the way we think about human identity and purpose and where history is headed. How we answer the question of origins reveals what we think about our worth, our purpose, and our sense of obligation to one another and to God.

In contrast to the secular worldviews, the biblical storyline gives each human life meaning and relevance by rooting us in God's purposes in creation. Creation is part of a larger story that moves to a culmination of God's purposes and a complete revelation of his character. This larger story moves along four major epochs: creation, fall, redemption, and consummation—each like a major movement in a grand symphony. We, that is, humanity, are all characters in this story. If our lives are to have proper meaning, we must know our place in this narrative and understand how we can be part of God's purpose of glorifying himself in creation.

But, if the narrative does not begin with creation, then the world itself exists by some explanation other than God, and the biblical narrative ends.[1] If we lose this perspective, we not only risk but ensure our fall into theological error. By establishing God as Creator, and we as his creatures, we find purpose and order in the universe. We exist for God and for his glory. The entire Christian worldview hangs on the Creator/creature distinction.

Although creation itself reveals God and leaves us without excuse to refuse to believe and worship our Creator (Rom. 1:20), we still require special revelation to believe *in him* because of our sin. Paul claimed that creation testifies of the Creator, and we the creatures should see God's invisible attributes in the things that are made (Rom. 1:18–32). But Paul did not forget the effect of the fall, which left every part of us corrupted by sin (Gen. 6:5–6; Rom. 3:10–18). Our sin disables us from clearly seeing what should be evident in creation. Therefore, we absolutely depend upon special revelation and the Word of God to make us see what we otherwise cannot and will not see.

The Apostles' Creed is dependent upon the clarity of God's Word. The creed establishes central Christian doctrines and thus the entire framework of the Christian worldview. In understanding the first line of the creed, "I believe in God, the Father Almighty, Maker of heaven and earth," we can answer the fundamental questions for any worldview: Who? What? When? Where? How? Why?

Who?

Scripture answers the "Who?" question immediately. In the beginning *God created* (Gen. 1:1–31). This God is none other than the triune God—Father, Son, and Holy Spirit. Revealed to Israel as Yahweh, the Lord God is the maker of heaven and earth (Gen. 2:4; Ex. 20:11; 2 Kings 19:15; 2 Chron. 2:12; Neh. 9:6; Ps. 121:2; Isa. 37:16; Jer. 32:17). Psalm 115:15 (NASB) says,

> May you be blessed of the LORD,
> Maker of heaven and earth.

Isaiah poetically wrote:

> It is he who sits above the circle of the earth,
> and its inhabitants are like grasshoppers;
> who stretches out the heavens like a curtain,
> and spreads them like a tent to dwell in. (Isa. 40:22)

> To whom then will you compare me,
> that I should be like him? says the Holy One . . .
> Who created these?
> He who brings out their host by number,
> calling them all by name;
> by the greatness of his might . . .
> not one is missing. (Isa. 40:25–26)

> Have you not known? Have you not heard?
> The LORD is the everlasting God,
> the Creator of the ends of the earth.
> He does not faint or grow weary;
> his understanding is unsearchable. (Isa. 40:28)

God also revealed himself as Creator to Job, to humble and to encourage him. In Job 38:1–7 God spoke to Job,

> Then the LORD answered Job out of the whirlwind
>   and said:
> "Who is this that darkens counsel by words without
>   knowledge?
> Dress for action like a man;
> I will question you, and you make it known to me.
> Where were you when I laid the foundation of the earth?
> Tell me, if you have understanding.
> Who determined its measurements—surely you know!
> Or who stretched the line upon it?
> On what were its bases sunk,
>   or who laid its cornerstone,
> when the morning stars sang together
> and all the sons of God shouted for joy?"

"Where were you?" God said to Job (38:4). There is no more humbling question.

> "Have you ever in your life commanded the morning,
> And caused the dawn to know its place?" (38:12 NASB)

Job was appropriately mute. But God continued,

> "Can you lift up your voice to the clouds,
> that a flood of waters may cover you?" (38:34)

> "Do you know when the mountain goats give birth?
> Do you observe the calving of the does?" (39:1)

"Do you give the horse his might?
Do you clothe his neck with a mane?" (39:19)

"Is it by your understanding that the hawk soars
and spreads his wings toward the south?" (39:26)

But as God said to Job, "Where were you when I laid the foundation of the earth?" (Job 38:4). Job finally responded,

"Behold, I am insignificant; what can I reply to You?
I lay my hand on my mouth.
Once I have spoken, and I will not answer;
Even twice, and I will add nothing more." (40:3–5 NASB)

Job believed in God the Father Almighty, Maker of heaven and earth. We, too, stand with Job and the Apostles' Creed and are humbled in the presence of our Creator.

Contrary to anything remotely supernatural, Darwinism and other secular origin theories begin with the material world to explain the existence of the universe. In *Darwin's Dangerous Idea*, atheist Daniel Dennett recalls a song he loved to sing during his childhood that he now finds fanciful. As Dennett explains, "One of my favorite songs was, 'Tell Me Why.'" The song's basic sentiment is that God made everything.

Dennett says, "This straightforward, sentimental declaration still brings a lump to my throat. So sweet, so innocent, so reassuring—a vision of life—and then along comes Darwin and spoils the picnic." He explains what happens when we follow Darwin's logic,

The sweet, simple version of the song, taken literally, is one that most of us have outgrown . . . *that* God is, like Santa

Claus, a myth of childhood, not anything a sane, undeluded adult could literally believe in. *That* God must either be turned into a symbol for something less concrete or abandoned altogether.[2]

For Darwinists this logic is inescapable. Darwinism begins with the material world, not with God as Creator. Denying God as Creator destroys everything else Christians affirm. Dennett went so far as to call Darwinism a "universal acid." As Dennett explains, he and his friends in junior high school came up with this category of a universal acid—an acid that was so powerful that it would burn through anything that sought to contain it. As it burned through the container, it would burn through the room in which the container was found. It would then burn through the school. Then the entire building would be dissolved into absolute nothingness. The acid would travel into the core of the earth until there was nothing else for it to destroy (you can imagine junior high boys amazed at this idea). Dennett says Darwinism is like a universal ideological acid. It burns through everything, leaving nothing. This is why Darwinism and nihilism go hand in hand. Without God as the ultimate starting point, we have no purpose in life, and the universe is a mere accident.

What?

God, the Father Almighty is the One who created. But what did God create? Scripture answers this second fundamental question: "the heavens and the earth" (Gen. 1:1). The entire universe, or cosmos, fills us with wonder and awe at the Creator. He created animal, plant, fungi, protozoa, and eukaryotic kingdoms. He created elephants and frogs, deciduous and coniferous forests, mushrooms, bacteria, and even the smallest amoeba.

Such biodiversity testifies to God's delight in the complexity of the universe; and it brings him great glory.

Some of God's diverse creation delight the eye; other things strike fear into the heart of man. William Blake testifies to this diversity in two poems in his series *Songs of Innocence and Experience*. First Blake reflects on "The Lamb":

> Little Lamb, who made thee
> Dost thou know who made thee,
> Gave thee life, and bid thee feed
> By the stream and o'er the mead;
> Gave thee clothing of delight,
> Softest clothing, woolly, bright;
> Gave thee such a tender voice . . .
> Little Lamb, I'll tell thee:
> He is called by thy name,
> For He calls Himself a Lamb
> He is meek, and He is mild,
> He became a little child.
> I a child, and thou a lamb,
> We are called by His name.
> Little Lamb, God bless thee!
> Little Lamb, God bless thee![3]

Blake personifies himself as a child—a child observing nature. He understands that the lamb requires an origin. At the same time, the same Creator behind the simple, gentle lamb, must also be the Creator behind the magnificent, ferocious tiger.

> TIGER, tiger, burning bright
> In the forests of the night,

What immortal hand or eye
Could frame thy fearful symmetry?[4]

Indeed, God made the tiger as well as the lamb. He made the hawk and the sparrow. He made the tender and the tough, the ferocious and the feeble. He made all that populates the earth. And his glory is in them all.

Nihilism, which stands radically opposed to the Apostles' Creed and the Christian worldview, suggests that life has no meaning and the creation has no purpose. Propelled by random, meaningless forces of nature, the universe remains entirely amoral. For nihilists there is no creator, rather, "In the beginning, was a force." But, a force cannot explain the existence of universal moral absolutes. Nihilism suggests that murder, rape, and oppression are not wrong but rather unfortunate happenings with no moral significance. But Christians cannot affirm such self-evident nonsense. We affirm from the outset that God created the world and gave us morality for our flourishing.

This fact is woven into man's very nature. As Moses wrote, God created us in his image (Gen. 1:26–27, 9:6). Humans are themselves creatures but creatures unlike any other. Possessing God's image, or *imago dei*, allows us to think about the things we are considering. Being made in God's image means we have the faculties needed to think about the Creator, for we reflect God's ability to reason. Being made in God's image also allows us to worship God, for we understand our dependency upon him. Humans are also the only creatures able to *consciously* rebel. For in this world you find not only the creature made in God's image, but after Genesis 3, you find the creature's image marred by sin. Sin and its consequences leave this world crying out for redemption.

When?

We now understand the *who* and *what* of creation, but *when* did God create the heavens and the earth? To answer that question, we must understand that time, space, and matter can only exist together. Thus, prior to creation, God was outside of time, space, and matter. God alone existed as the Trinity. But the first line of Scripture tells us that God created "in the beginning." God created matter at a particular time, and he created space for the matter to exist.

The biblical narrative has a great deal to do with time. Time begins at creation. The creation and subsequent fall of mankind set up the promise for which Christ would come in the fullness of time. The narrative also looks forward toward a new age when time shall be no more.

Where?

A popular denial of God and all of Christianity, including the Apostles' Creed, comes from Carl Sagan, the late scientist of Cornell University. In his 1980 mini-series called *Cosmos*, Sagan begins every episode by reiterating, "The cosmos is all that ever was, or is, or ever shall be." This statement manifests a worldview of naturalistic materialism. Instead of beginning with God as Creator, naturalists begin and end with the cosmos itself, which leaves the door open to any other cosmos of which we are unaware.

But by dignifying *this* material world, Christians are not left wishing for some counterfactual reality in another world. *This* is our Father's world. Scripture gives us no reason to think that God created some other universe. Our universe is the space that God created. The Bible continually points to *this* universe as our constant frame of reference for the biblical story. Indeed, the promises of a new heaven and a new earth use language that only refers to this universe. Therefore, speculation about other universes is not helpful within a coherent Christian worldview. He created this world that could be, and should be, studied. Thus, Christianity affirms the intelligible foundation from which the natural sciences could emerge. For if the world were not intelligible, we could not investigate it and would have no rational foundation for scientific inquiry.

How?

Science cannot answer the question *how* God created the universe. Once again, we must rely on the clear teaching of Scripture. Scripture not only teaches us that God is the author of all creation, it also shows God's *agent* in creation—his Word. Each creative act begins with "God *said*" (Gen. 1:3, 6, 9, 11, 14, 20, 24, 26). His Word is the perfect representation of his will and of his glory, not lacking in any aspect or dimensionality. Therefore, God created by the power of his Word, out of nothing. His speech was not merely a collection of verbs and nouns, but rather a person who "became flesh and dwelt among us" (John 1:14).

Echoing the creation narrative of Genesis, John began his gospel with "in the beginning was the Word, and the Word was with God, and the Word was God. He was in the beginning with God. All things came into being through Him, and apart from Him nothing came into being that has come into being" (John 1:1–3 NASB). John's concise yet profound theology explains how God created with the same Word by which he redeems us. God's Word spoke all things into existence, and God's Word took on human flesh to redeem his people.

By becoming flesh and redeeming his people, Jesus earned the right to sit at the Father's right hand and receive due honor.

> "Worthy are you, our Lord and God,
>
> to receive glory and honor and power,
>
> for you created all things,
>
> and by your will they existed and were created." (Rev. 4:11)

God receives praise for authorship, Jesus for his agency.

Similarly, Paul reflected on Jesus' agency in creation when he wrote, "He is the image of the invisible God, the firstborn of all creation. For by Him all things were created, both in the heavens and on earth, visible and invisible; whether thrones or dominions or rulers or authorities—all things have been created through Him and for Him" (Col. 1:15–16 NASB). The "Him" refers to Jesus, God's Son. Jesus created all things, and all things were created "for Him."

Why?

The words "created . . . for Him" in Colossians 1:16 show us the end for which God created the world. Scripture teaches that God does all things for his own purpose and his own glory:

> He chose us in him before the foundation of the world, that we should be holy and blameless before him. In love he predestined us for adoption to himself as sons through Jesus Christ, according to the purpose of his will, to the praise of his glorious grace, with which he has blessed us in the Beloved. In him we have redemption through his blood, the forgiveness of our trespasses, according to the riches of his grace, which he lavished upon us, in all wisdom and insight making known to us the mystery of his will, according to his purpose, which he set forth in Christ as a plan for the fullness of time, to unite all things in him, things in heaven and things on earth. (Eph. 1:4–10)

Our God is in the heavens;
    he does all that he pleases. (Ps. 115:3)

The heavens declare the glory of God,
    and the sky above proclaims his handiwork. (Ps. 19:1)

As the supreme being over all things, God's primary determination must be to display his own glory. John Calvin claimed that the cosmos is the theater of God's glory. Calvin is right, for the entire created order exists for one great purpose: to display the glory of God through the *redemption* of sinners through Jesus Christ the Son. Creation leads to new creation. Thus, God ultimately created the cosmos for redemptive purposes. The agent of creation becomes the agent of redemption. One day, the agent of redemption will become the agent of new creation.

Our hearts ache to return to Eden. We ache to return to Genesis 2, as if Genesis 3 never happened, but we do so in vain. Going backward is impossible and would not be for God's greater glory. Rather, we go forward. We strive for the new heaven and new earth, not the old. We groan with the rest of creation, awaiting the return of Christ and the fullness of God's kingdom (Rom. 8:22). From Genesis to Revelation we will see the glory of God. Then, finally, one day we will hear him say, "Behold, I am making all things new" (Rev. 21:5; cf. 2 Cor. 5:17).

This promise of new creation ought to bring comfort to the Christian. God takes responsibility for his creation, and he will see it through to glory. God will bring his children home by his providential care. God's provision is perhaps never more sweetly summarized than in the first article of Luther's *Small Catechism of 1529*:

I believe that God has created me and all that exists; that he has given me and still sustains my body and soul, all my limbs and senses, my reason and all the faculties of my mind, together with food and clothing, house and home, family and property; that he provides me daily and abundantly with all the necessities of life, protects me from all danger, and preserves me from all evil.

Do you so believe? We believe in God, the Father Almighty, Maker of heaven and earth.

CHAPTER THREE

JESUS CHRIST, HIS ONLY SON, OUR LORD

Christians are defined by one primary mark: we believe in and are disciples of the Lord Jesus Christ. Whatever beliefs may separate churches and denominations, a true Christian is someone who has repented of his or her sin and embraced Christ as the only Lord and Savior. We are a people of Christ. In fact, we instinctually use language such as "Christ-centered" to describe our worship and our lives. This commitment to Christ is not just a modern evangelical phenomenon; it is also reflected in the ancient faith of the Apostles' Creed. The largest portion of the creed is devoted to Christ. As a matter of fact, we should see the Apostles' Creed as a confession of Christ with an introduction and a conclusion. The creed chronicles the storyline of

Jesus, from his conception by the Holy Spirit to his elevation and his ascension—from his exaltation to his promised return as king.

One thing to note immediately is how the creed confronts today's tendency toward theological minimalism. It is not enough to simply say "I love Jesus" or "I follow Jesus." Many who say they love Jesus and follow Jesus do not follow Jesus as he has revealed himself in Scripture. As the confession reminds us, we must confess that we believe in "Jesus Christ, His only Son, our Lord"—the Jesus whose true identity and mission is revealed in Scripture.

We must identify who this Lord is whom we worship—this Savior who has redeemed us from our sin. Regrettably, even in Christian churches, a superficial Christology sometimes permeates the church, its worship, and its witness. Some of this spirituality has devolved into unabashedly false doctrine. Some want a Jesus who is a great teacher but not the Son of the Father. Some want Jesus as savior but not Lord.

We're living in this strange time in which it appears to people that heresy is exhilarating. Just as in the early centuries of the church, it takes courage to be an orthodox Christian. It takes courage to confess the "faith that was once for all delivered to the saints" (Jude 3). It takes courage to believe the orthodox faith of the church, rooted in Scripture—but confessional courage is exhilarating. Throughout Christian history many believers have faced persecution, imprisonment, and even death for the sake of the gospel. Their courage in the face of immense adversity should inspire us.

Years ago, I traveled to Washington, DC, to participate in a theological debate of the Christian faith. It was an invitation I could not let go. I felt duty bound to accept it. They were finding it very difficult to find someone who would actually stand for the orthodox faith, and I felt that I should do it. It was one of those debates that (as I got into it) I discovered was set up for something other than an honest exchange of ideas. It was an opportunity for the faith to be humiliated. And in the midst of this very hostile audience, I prayed that the Lord would give me some opportunity in an unexpected way to break through the mechanism of this debate and to give a testimony to the gospel that would not just be the answer to a question but would somehow be used by the Holy Spirit to open eyes and hearts.

This particular debate allowed questions from the audience. For most of the debate, that was a disaster. At one moment, however, it was accidently glorious. A man stood up and identified himself as holding two PhDs—one in astrophysics and the other in something similar. We knew, therefore, he must be smart. Furthermore, he declared, he had studied theology, and then he said that he was a senior scientist with NASA. He said, "Dr. Mohler, I am just so tired of all this theology. I'm tired of all this doctrine. Every time you get asked a question, you respond with a theological answer."

And I said, "Sir, you'll notice the program says, 'A Theological Debate.' Someone with two PhDs should understand what that word means."

And then he said something that gave me all I needed. He exclaimed, "Dr. Mohler, I am so tired of all this doctrine and theology! I'm a Christian, and I want nothing to do with doctrine and theology. All I want is Jesus Christ."

It was as if the runway was cleared. All the traffic went away, and the clouds parted. I was cleared for takeoff. I said, "Sir, do you think there was a mailbox in Judea that said, 'Christ, Jesus'? Do you think that's his last name? You just made a theological statement! You, who want nothing to do with theology, by naming the name Jesus Christ have made a profoundly theological statement.

You say that all you want is Jesus Christ, but do you know what you're saying? You're declaring Jesus to be 'the Anointed One of God, the Messiah.' Christ is not a surname. It is a title. Jesus Christ is not merely a name; it is a theological proposition. It is the claim that all the promises given to Israel are fulfilled in this one incarnate man. His name, Jesus, means 'The Lord Saves.'"

That moment in the debate reveals the inevitability of all statements about Christ to bear theological significance. Indeed, to say "all I want is Jesus Christ" amounts to a *profound* theological declaration. The Christian faith cherishes the truth that Jesus Christ is God's only Son—the Lord. This is actually the sum and substance of the Christian faith. The shortest and most universal declaration of any Christian is simply this: "Jesus is Lord."

When it comes to answering the central question, "Who is Christ?" it is Jesus himself who forces the question. Jesus asked his disciples, "Who do *you* say that I am?" (Matt. 16:15). Later Jesus again asked the question, "What do you think about the Christ?" (Matt. 22:42). In reality there is no more important question than this. It defines who we are. On the Day of Judgment, we will be defined by our Christology. We will meet the Christ either as Savior, or we will meet him as Judge. We face the temptation of theological minimalism and confusion. We want to say something other than what the church knows through Scripture. But we must always confess with Scripture and with the creed: "I believe in Jesus Christ, his only Son, our Lord."

Jesus the Christ

An angel appeared to Joseph to tell him that the child who had been conceived in Mary by the Holy Spirit would be called Jesus, "for he will save his people from their sins" (Matt. 1:21). Later another assembly of angels appeared to shepherds in the fields of Bethlehem and proclaimed, "Fear not, for behold, I bring you good news of great joy that will be for all the people. For unto you is born this day in the city of David a Savior, who is Christ the Lord" (Luke 2:10–11). We believe in Jesus the Christ, the anointed one, the Messiah, the one who was promised to Israel, the one who fulfills all these promises and so much more. Calling him "Jesus Christ" unmistakably emphasizes that he was and is our Savior. At the mention of his name—if we understand its meaning—we confess that we are a people who are pitiable and weak, defenseless and helpless. We need a Savior. We need Christ, the Lord.

And in Jesus Christ we have all the Savior we need: the one who saves us from our sins and saves us from hell. The grand story of how that takes place is narrated in successive statements of the creed, but we can't even get into the story without confessing what the angels said on that night to those shepherds: "Unto you is born this day in the city of David a Savior, who is Christ the Lord" (Luke 2:11).

Salvation in Christ Alone

The Lord saves through his Messiah. This idea is a primary element of early Christian apostolic preaching. In Acts 2:36 we find that on the day of Pentecost, Peter said, "Let all the house of Israel therefore know for certain that God has made him both Lord and Christ, this Jesus whom you crucified." Notice also that at the center of this apostolic preaching is the assurance that this was God's plan. Just before this statement, Peter had preached,

> Men of Israel, hear these words: Jesus of Nazareth, a man attested to you by God with mighty works and wonders and

signs that God did through him in your midst, as you your-selves know—this Jesus, delivered up according to the definite plan and foreknowledge of God, you crucified and killed by the hands of lawless men. God raised him up, loosing the pangs of death, because it was not possible for him to be held by it. (Acts 2:22–24)

All these truths will be recited and affirmed a number of times throughout Acts and detailed in the creed. In Acts 3 as Peter and John are going up into the temple, they are confronted with a man who is lame from his mother's womb. Peter tells the man, "I have no silver and gold, but what I do have I give to you. In the name of Jesus Christ of Nazareth, rise up and walk!" (v. 6). Notice this command was not given merely in the name of Jesus, but in the name of *Jesus Christ*. It's Jesus' messiahship that is at the heart of his saving work.

In Peter's second sermon in Acts, he preaches:

But what God foretold by the mouth of all the prophets, that his Christ would suffer, he thus fulfilled. Repent therefore, and turn back, that your sins may be blotted out, that times of refreshing may come from the presence of the Lord, and that he may send the Christ [notice the specificity, the clarity of his testimony here] appointed for you, Jesus, whom heaven must receive until the time for restoring all the things about which God spoke by the mouth of his holy prophets long ago. (3:18–21)

We are told that Peter was filled with the Holy Spirit and, speaking after his arrest to the Sanhedrin, said,

"Rulers of the people and elders, if we are being examined today concerning a good deed done to a crippled man, by what means this man has been healed, let it be known to all of you and to all the people of Israel that by the name of Jesus Christ of Nazareth, whom you crucified, whom God raised from the dead—by him this man is standing before you well. This Jesus is the stone that was rejected by you, the builders, which has become the cornerstone. And there is salvation in no one else, for there is no other name under heaven given among men by which we must be saved." (Acts 4:8–12)

The audacity of this in the context of the Judaism of the day is breathtaking. It is dangerous to speak these things without reflecting upon what they mean. With his life on the line, Peter boldly proclaimed the unique exclusivity of Jesus Christ. Only through the Christ can we be saved; only by his name will we come into God's presence.

The Quest for the Historical Jesus

Human ingenuity would not have arrived at the conclusion that Jesus is the Christ. Human investigation could not discern this. We need this reminder because, especially in the twenty-first century, there have arisen movements within institutional Christianity to try to find some other way of defining who Jesus is. Much of this can be attributed to the infamous quest for the historical Jesus that began in the nineteenth century. The idea that we can just dispense with the biblical materials altogether and try to reconstruct a Jesus from history is folly. Christians do not gather in the name of Jesus Christ, whom we have come to know by the means of historical investigation excluding

Scripture. That is the futile ambition pursued by those who want to minimize and humanize Jesus so that he is no longer the Christ—the Son of the Living God—but merely Jesus the teacher.

Central to this quest for the historical Jesus is a distinction between what is called "the Jesus of history" and the "Christ of faith." But a dichotomy between the Jesus of history and the Jesus of Scripture is false and dangerous. We are not Christians if we do not believe that the historical Jesus is also the Christ of our faith plainly held out to us in the fourfold testimony of the Gospels. Moreover, we are still dead in our trespasses and sins if the Jesus of history is not the Christ of faith. As Paul would tell us, "we are of all people most to be pitied" (1 Cor. 15:19) if the Jesus of history is not the Christ of faith—raised bodily from the dead on the third day. We live joyfully and we pursue holiness because we believe that the Jesus of history recorded in the Gospels, proclaimed by the apostles, and found in the New Testament is the Christ of faith—Jesus Christ.

George Tyrrell, speaking of the quest for the historical Jesus, once aptly noted, "The Christ that [these scholars see], looking back through nineteen centuries of Catholic darkness, is only the reflection of a Liberal Protestant face, seen at the bottom of a deep well."[1] What Tyrrell was saying was that the "historical" Jesus always ends up reflecting the values and biases of the scholars investigating him. These historically reconstructed portraits of Jesus are refashioned into the image of theological liberalism. This is one of the greatest attractions of heresy—to have a Jesus who is more like us. This Jesus might be more culturally acceptable, but he is certainly not the Christ, the Son of the Living God.

The quest for the historical Jesus and its attendant theological liberalism took new shape in a movement known as the Jesus Seminar. Led by the late Robert Funk, this academic guild decided that they were going to start yet another quest for the historical Jesus. Their work proceeded on the assumption that there is no supernatural revelation and that the canonical gospels were historically untrustworthy. But embedded within the gospel traditions are certain historical sources that might be boiled down to something that could finally be understood as the historical Jesus.

As incredible as it may seem, these scholars decided they would proceed through the four gospels verse by verse and assign a colored marble to each verse. A red marble meant they believed the statement or action of Jesus was authentic. The black marble represented inauthenticity. The gray marble meant "probably not authentic" and the pink marble meant "probably authentic." To no one's surprise there was rarely red on the table. Finally, the Jesus Seminar produced the color-coded publication of the Gospels, which consisted of predominantly black and gray text. In the end the only evaluation that can be made of the Jesus Seminar is that these scholars have figuratively lost their marbles. They have fashioned a Jesus of their own making, one who looks just like them.

While it is easy to condemn the Jesus Seminar's tampering with Scripture, we must remember that we all face the same temptation. We read the Gospels and selectively composite texts that create a Jesus who values what we value. We must confess our complete dependence upon the revelation of God in Scripture lest we preach some other Jesus, some other Christ.

Jesus is the supernatural Savior. We know this by means of a supernatural revelation. To a good number of people we will meet, that means we believe in the supernatural and thus are to be discounted in a world committed to naturalistic materialism. That is the scandal we must bear. That is the Jesus we worship: Jesus the Christ.

His Only Son

"I believe in God, the Father Almighty, Maker of heaven and earth, and in Jesus Christ, his only Son, our Lord." His only Son—the notion of the Messiah being the "Son of God" is rooted in the Old Testament. God, promising David that his son, Solomon, would build the temple, said, "I will be to him a father, and he shall be to me a son" (2 Sam. 7:14). Thus, the notion of "sonship" was always connected to Davidic kingship. The Messiah would be both king of Israel and a New David, thus he would be the Son of God.

More profoundly, however, Jesus is God's Son because he is the second person of the Trinity. Arguably the most profound aspect of the incarnation is that before the incarnation the Son was already the only begotten of the Father. The Nicene Creed uses clear, biblical language in order to communicate this notion, describing Jesus as the one who was eternally "begotten" and not "made." We must recognize that the Son is not a creature. No mere creature could save us. Jesus Christ is not a creature—he is the only begotten Son of the Father. Scripture clearly teaches the preexistence of the Son as the Son. The Son is sent. "God so loved the world, that he gave"—he sent—"his only Son" (John 3:16; Heb. 1:1–4).

After Jesus was baptized the Father spoke from heaven: "This is my beloved Son, with whom I am well pleased" (Matt. 3:17). By union with Christ through faith, we also are the sons and daughters of God. Jesus is the eternal Son of God. He is the only begotten Son of God. But, as Hebrews tells us, he is "bringing many sons to glory" (2:10), and it is by his atonement that we are adopted as sons and daughters of the most high. As the apostle Paul said, we are "fellow heirs with Christ" (Rom. 8:17). The only reason we can ever be called the adopted sons and daughters of God is because Jesus is, indeed, the only begotten Son of God.

Christ, Our Lord

"I believe in Jesus Christ, his only Son, our Lord." Philippians provides an incredible testimony to the fact that Jesus willingly took on human flesh in the incarnation to identify with sinful humanity. He came to save his people from their sins, and this led to the cross—not as an accident, not as an unexpected incident, but rather as God's predetermined plan—and Jesus willingly emptied himself. Not only did he condescend himself in order to take on the form of a man, but he willingly subjected himself to death for us. As a result, Christ became the Lord, the eternal Davidic king.

In Philippians, Paul wrote on account of Christ's cross work: "Therefore God has highly exalted him and bestowed on him the name that is above every name, so that at the name of Jesus every knee should bow, in heaven and on earth and under the earth, and every tongue confess that Jesus Christ is Lord, to the glory of God the Father" (2:9–11). This verse is the fulfillment of the promise in Isaiah 40:5, that the Christ would reveal the glory of God to all peoples. This doctrine is also the substance of the apostolic preaching: "Let all the house of Israel therefore know for certain that God has made him both Lord and Christ, this Jesus whom you crucified" (Acts 2:36).

Many resist the doctrine of Christ's lordship. The forms of resistance are many and complex. But the sinful heart loathes the lordship of Christ. For instance, one news story a few years ago from Tucson, Arizona, reflects this very fact.

> In Tucson's largest Episcopal Church, St. Phillips in the Hills, the creators of an alternative worship service called, "Come and See" are bucking tradition by rewriting what has become prescribed ways of worship. For the faithful that means that God isn't referred to as "Him" and references to the "Lord" are rare. "Lord has become a loaded word, conveying hierarchical power over things, which in what we have recorded in our sacred texts, is not who Jesus considered Himself to be," speaks St. Phillips Associate Rector, Susan Anderson Smith. St. Phillip's deacon, Thomas Lindell added, "The way our service reads, theology is that God is Love—period. Our service has done everything it can to get rid of power imagery. We do not pray as though we expect a big guy in the sky to come and fix everything."[2]

But this is exactly what we needed—for God to come and to fix everything, to send his beloved Son to save us from sin.

More commonly, most people simply assert that they do not need a lord. Some even claim that they can accept Christ as Savior but not as Lord. This assertion, however, is a complete misunderstanding of New Testament theology and an unbiblical separation of Christ's offices of Priest and King. Jesus himself asks in Luke 6:46, "Why do you call me 'Lord, Lord,' and not do what I tell you?" Salvation comes to those who confess that we desperately need a Savior, and at the same time that the Savior is "Christ the Lord" (Luke 2:11). In Romans 10:9 we are told that salvation comes to those who confess with their lips that Jesus Christ is Lord.

Heresies will come and go. Trials will come and go. But the church of the Lord Jesus will remain. His lordship endures even though we struggle to fully embrace his sovereignty in our every circumstance. But a day is coming when every knee shall bow, and every tongue shall confess "that Jesus Christ is Lord, to the glory of God the Father" (Phil. 2:11). And we are saved because, and only because, of Jesus Christ, God's only Son, our Lord.

CHAPTER FOUR

CONCEIVED OF THE HOLY SPIRIT, BORN OF THE VIRGIN MARY

For the whole of church history, Christians have preserved essential doctrines in and through their hymnody. For example, the doctrine of the virgin birth has populated several Christmas hymns: "Silent Night," "Hark the Herald Angels Sing," and "God Rest Ye Merry Gentlemen." These hymns, which represent many others, are pregnant with meaning and represent a necessary element of the Christian faith, without which the gospel does not save sinners. To some, however, the virgin birth and Christ's miraculous conception exemplify the supernatural scandal of Christianity. Modern skeptics like retired Episcopal bishop John Shelby Spong have argued that these doctrines are just evidence of the early church's invention of Christ's deity. The virgin birth is, Spong explains, the "entrance myth" to go with the resurrection, the "exit myth." Like Spong, many consider themselves far too sophisticated to believe in things like blood redemption or a virgin birth. These doctrines remain a foreign concept to many, a cultural symbol to some, and a point of division for others.

My election as president of the Southern Baptist Theological Seminary came during a divisive and vitriolic time for the Southern Baptist Convention. Theological orthodoxy and doctrinal fidelity hung in the balance as warring factions sought to control the future of the convention. In the midst of that controversy, the issue of the virgin birth arose. One prominent leader of the liberal faction said that a professor of theology "who might also be led by the Scripture not to believe in the virgin birth should not be fired." In other words, any teacher who denied the virgin birth remained in orthodoxy so long as they believed that position to arise from the Scriptures. Led by the Scripture not to believe in the virgin birth? What kind of evasion is that? The sentence does not even make sense. The Scriptures teach nothing less than the virgin birth of Jesus Christ. Indeed, without such a birth there is no gospel! A Christian who doesn't believe in the virgin birth is in eternal peril, for the one in whom he believes is not the One who is testified in the Scriptures.

The Apostles' Creed, therefore, has included the virgin birth for good reason—it is true, it is essential, and it is glorious. As the creed suggests, Jesus Christ, the seed of the woman whose heel would strike the serpent and reverse the curse, was conceived by a sovereign act of God and born of a virgin. The church, I hope to show you, must affirm the virgin birth because it rests at the foundation of other critical doctrines. Without the virgin birth, Christ is not God. If Christ was not conceived by the Holy Spirit, then he must have a human father, and thus he is not divine. Also, without the virgin birth, the gospel does not provide salvation. If the virgin birth is a lie, then Jesus could never reverse the curse and save sinners. Moreover, if Christians deny the virgin birth, and treat the conception of the Holy Spirit as a myth, then they threaten a whole range of other Christian doctrines: the truthfulness of Scripture, the humanity of Christ, the sinlessness of Christ, and the nature of grace. Christians today must affirm the virgin birth of Christ—indeed, the Christian faith and the Bible on which that faith stands demand it.

Soundings from Church History

The Church Fathers

The Apostles' Creed reminds modern Christians that our faith finds deep roots in the history of the church. With more than two thousand years of thoughtful interaction with Scripture, church history offers an abundance of theological material with which to address modern theological questions. In fact, one would not have to look far into church history to see that the virgin birth was central to the proclamation of the early church fathers. Justin Martyr, Irenaeus, Tertullian, Basil, Jerome, and Augustine all wrote about the importance of the virgin birth. The church has consistently understood the virgin birth as central to the proclamation of the Scriptures.

The church fathers explained, expounded, and applied the doctrine of the virgin birth so that the church would understand its significance. They were some of the first to see a three-way connection between the nature of Christ's conception, the nature of Christ, and the work of Christ. In other words, the nature of Christ's conception is central to the entire story of redemption. The church fathers understood that for Jesus to save, Jesus must be both God and man; and in order to achieve this union between God and humanity, Jesus must be conceived by the Holy Spirit and born of the Virgin Mary. Jesus only serves as a perfect substitute and efficacious offering for sin if he is both fully God and fully man. Irenaeus, commenting on a heresy that denies the virginal conception, noted the significance of the human and divine nature of Jesus' conception:

> For He would not have been one truly possessing flesh and blood, by which He redeemed us, unless He had summed up in Himself the ancient formation of Adam [humanity]. . . . Vain also are the Ebionites . . . who do not choose to understand that the Holy Ghost came upon Mary, and the power of the Most High did overshadow her (Luke 1:35): wherefore also what was generated is a holy thing, and the Son of the Most High God the Father of all, who effected the incarnation of this being, and showed forth a new [kind of] generation; that as by the former generation we inherited death, so by this new generation we might inherit life.[1]

In this passage Irenaeus makes a connection between the nature of Christ's conception (conceived by the Spirit and born of Mary), the nature of Christ (both fully God and fully man), and the work of Christ (perfect human representative and last Adam; 1 Cor. 15:22). The church fathers understood that without a proper understanding of Jesus in the womb one would never understand the significance of Christ on the cross. The nature of Christ's conception is central to the gospel.

The Enlightenment and Classical Liberalism

Although the church has affirmed the virgin birth of Christ for two thousand years, in the last two hundred years, some have labeled the virgin birth a scandal. The Enlightenment and the rise of liberal theology account for this radical departure from the orthodoxy of church history—indeed, few other events in church history have played such a substantial role in the alteration of the historic faith. For some modern theologians the doctrine of the virgin birth has been an embarrassment. During the Enlightenment, theologians and philosophers utilized human reason independent of divine revelation and historic orthodoxy. As a result theologians began to question the validity of the inherited orthodoxy. Scripture became a mere historic document, susceptible to all the criticism of any historic piece of literature that lacks a divine authoritative status. Along with the text of Scripture, every major biblical doctrine was reshaped and reformulated along rationalistic lines. Christology in general, and the virgin birth specifically, experienced the most austere reshaping as a result of this new "Age of Reason."

The German philosopher G. E. Lessing demonstrated the Enlightenment's effects on the Christian and historic orthodoxy. He suggested that historical events could never provide the type of knowledge needed for rational religion. He called history "an ugly broad ditch" between the past and the present. Lessing meant that we can never really know what happened in the past. No one, he claimed, could cross that "ugly ditch" into the past.

But the Bible reveals the past to us. Once again, we understand just how dependent we are upon the Scriptures. Without

the Bible, we would not even know our own stories. The Bible—
God's inspired and totally truthful Word to us—crosses Lessing's
"ugly ditch" for us.

The Enlightenment and its effect on theology produced a
divide between historical orthodoxy and the new liberal understanding of theology. These two rival visions of Christianity
divided over the role of the supernatural. Either the God of the
Bible exists, and he acts unilaterally in history to reveal himself,
or he does not exist, and his self-revelation remains a Christian
myth. If God exists and acts in supernatural ways, then the
Christian need no longer worry about the "ugly broad ditch"
of history because God himself bridges the past and the present through his revelation in Scripture. To the Enlightenment
thinker, God's revelation in his Word and in Jesus was not supernatural, inerrant, or infallible. And through the denial of the
supernatural, this new intellectual movement laid the foundation for theological liberalism.

In the nineteenth and twentieth centuries, Protestant
Liberalism continued to repudiate supernatural beliefs like the
virgin birth of Christ. Friedrich Schleiermacher, the father of
theological liberalism, refused to speak of Christ and salvation
in terms of the supernatural; for him, salvation did not require
a supernatural intervention like the virgin birth. David Strauss
suggested that the New Testament, an artifact of history, represents a primitive expression of religion—an expression rooted in
myth and mysticism. Adolf von Harnack attempted to separate
religious dogma (the "husk") from the practical consequences
(the "kernel") of Christianity. He rejected the discussions about
the nature of Christ and the significance of his virgin birth—
after all, Jesus was ultimately a religious reformer and prophet.
Furthermore, Rudolph Bultmann taught that the New Testament

was nothing more than a collection of myths with existential relevance. The Bible, he suggested, must go through a process of "demythologization" whereby existential truth comes to the surface by whittling away myths like the virgin birth. Then, oddly enough, Wolfhart Pannenberg, one of the most influential theologians of the twentieth century, believed in the historic resurrection of Christ but not the virgin birth. In all its iterations, Protestant Liberalism of the last two centuries has tended to reject the supernatural, unilateral act of God in the virgin birth of Jesus.

Liberalism believed that the virgin birth was a humiliating supernatural assertion, and Protestant Liberalism tried to save the Christian faith from this embarrassing claim. Skeptics of the virgin birth, if consistent, must also doubt all the other supernatural elements in the Gospels like the presence of miracles or the empty tomb. In the fourth century Augustine prophetically addressed the heart of embarrassment found in much modern theology:

> So what do the so-called Wise and Prudent think of this great miracle? Well they prefer to think of it as a nice story rather than a hard fact. So, when it comes to Christ's appearing as man and God—clearly a divine consideration—they run into trouble. They think it beneath them to believe that there are things that aren't human; that there are in fact things that are divine. . . . To them it's just plain embarrassing that God should walk around in a silly, ill-fitting body. To us, of course, it's a genuinely encouraging sight. To put it another way, which'll truly appear perverse to the Unwise and Imprudent, the more impossible the virgin birth of a human being appears to them, the more divine it seems to us.[2]

During the time of Augustine, the virgin birth had become a scandalous doctrine, but Augustine understood that the true and faithful church will always believe the teachings of Scripture.

The Testimony of Scripture

Against the pronouncements of some modern theologians, the Gospels shamelessly portray the birth of Jesus as a miraculous and supernatural intervention by God. Matthew and Luke provide the clearest substantiations of the virgin birth, and the church has good reason to trust these accounts historically. Many scholars have noted the "Hebraic" personality of these gospel accounts, which means that these divine descriptions were not later first-century attempts by Christians to fortify doctrine relating to the divinity of Christ. Also, even the historical-critical liberal scholar, Adolf Harnack, admitted that Luke was a "trustworthy" and "genuinely historical" source.[3] However, while a careful analysis of the historicity of the Gospel accounts can help Christians see the reliability of Scripture, the dependability of Scripture must ultimately rest on the doctrine of inspiration. The Gospels, as a result, provided the strongest evidence for the virgin birth because they represent the accurate message of God to the church.

Both Matthew and Luke support the virginal conception of Jesus. Matthew says, "Before they came together she was found to be with child from the Holy Spirit" (Matt. 1:18). Mary fulfilled the prophecy of Isaiah 7:14 and 9:6–7 according to the Gospel writer: "Behold, the virgin shall conceive and bear a son, and they shall call his name Immanuel" (Matt. 1:23). Luke, in his narrative, emphasizes the fact that Mary was a virgin by repeating it three times. The angel Gabriel came "to a virgin" and "the virgin's name was Mary" (Luke 1:27). Then Mary replies to the angel, "I am a virgin" (Luke 1:34). Luke also provided greater detail about the role of the Holy Spirit. He explained, "The Holy Spirit will come upon you, and the power of the Most High will overshadow you; therefore, the child to be born will be called holy—the Son of God" (Luke 1:35). The Gospels feature both the virginity of Mary and the miraculous conception by the Holy Spirit.

Understood in light of salvation history, these Gospel accounts of the virgin birth satisfy the Old Testament yearning for a savior. God made a promise in Genesis 3:15 to annihilate the one who brought corruption, and, in the birth of Jesus, God accomplished his promises to redeem his people, destroy sin, and usher in a new creation. Jesus was the seed of the woman whose heel would strike the serpent and reverse the curse. Ironically Eve seemed to think the birth of Cain would result in the end of the curse (Gen. 4:1). But no child conceived in this manner could reverse the curse because no child conceived as Cain was conceived would be without Adam's inherited and imputed sin. In order that the death of Christ might fully atone for sin, he had to be fully God and fully man—born of the Holy Spirit through the virgin Mary. Jesus offers salvation to the world as the perfect representative on behalf of humanity.

Also, Mary and Joseph are models of how to receive the virgin birth by faith. When Joseph found out about the pregnancy of his betrothed, as an upright man he did not want to humiliate her. Not desiring to prosecute her, he tried to put her away privately. Then, when the angel appeared to Joseph and explained that this child within Mary had been conceived of the Holy Spirit, he believed. He did exactly what the Lord told him: "Do not fear to take Mary as your wife" (Matt. 1:20). Also, an angel visited Mary and announced to her that God had chosen her as a vessel for the birth of Immanuel. Mary responded, "Behold, I am the servant of the Lord; let it be to me according to your word" (Luke 1:38). Mary and Joseph modeled faith in God and faithfulness to his plan.

Doctrinal Significance of the Virgin Birth

As stated above, the virgin conception of Christ possesses significant doctrinal importance for the church; however, consider just three implications of the virgin birth. First, the virgin birth affirms the true identity of Christ as truly God and truly man. Wayne Grudem summarized the importance of this doctrine:

> God, in his wisdom, ordained a combination of human and divine influence in the birth of Christ, so that his full humanity would be evident to us from the fact of his ordinary human birth from a human mother, and his full deity would be evident from the fact of his conception in Mary's womb by the powerful work of the Holy Spirit.[4]

Jesus was not conceived by the will of a human man; rather, he was conceived of the Holy Spirit. The virgin birth makes possible the unity of the divine and the human.

Second, the virgin birth certainly points to the miracle by which this child is conceived without sin. According to Scripture, all those who descend from Adam receive the guilt of sin; however, Jesus does not descend from Adam and therefore he does not participate in that common condition (2 Cor. 5:21; Rom. 5:18–19). Peter Martyr Vermigli explained:

> All the descendants of the first Adam were subject to wrath and to sin without exception. But to spare the humanity of Christ from the common condition of our race, cleansing it from what is inherent in human nature, the Divine wisdom devised an amazing and wondrous plan. The Man who was joined to God and was to have both deity and humanity would be thus conceived. As the angel prophesied to the Virgin Mary, so the Holy Spirit descended on her. With matchless skill from her blood, already made pure by the most holy grace, He formed this unique and perfect man. Thus, by the God of mercy, the eternal Word assumed humanity. The womb of the Virgin Mary became the Divine furnace from which the Holy Spirit, out of sanctified flesh and blood, drew that body destined to be the obedient servant of no less a noble soul, thus none of the defects of fallen Adam were transmitted to Christ. Though the bodies of both were produced in a similar way, our first father was miraculously formed from the earth without the seed of man. But by the power of God, so was the second Adam.[5]

Third, the virgin birth accentuates the miraculous nature of God's redemption. Indeed, the virgin conception of Jesus can be explained only by the unilateral, sovereign act of God—this child is a gift from him. Humanity needed a perfect human savior, but humanity could never produce such a one. Carl F. H. Henry clarified: "Thus, from the fact that Jesus is 'born of the Virgin Mary,' it may be seen that the work of Incarnation and Reconciliation involves a definite intervening act on the part of

God himself. As Luther saw, a new beginning has to be made, a new creation initiated."[6] The birth of Christ emphasizes the need for God's supernatural intervention in history and displays God's initiative.

Those who deny, ignore, or explain away the virgin birth struggle to explain in any meaningful sense the divinity of the Son and the majesty of the incarnation. For this reason the miraculous birth of Christ stands at the vanguard of the New Testament; it has become a litmus test for orthodoxy:

> The virgin birth is posted on guard at the door of the mystery of Christmas; and none of us must think of hurrying past it. It stands on the threshold of the New Testament, blatantly supernatural, defying our rationalism, informing us that all that follows belongs to the same order as itself and that if we find it offensive there is no point in proceeding further.[7]

Protestant Liberalism provides an excellent example of this departure from the miraculous nature of Christ's birth. As a result, they relegate Christ to a wise sage or a moral revolutionary, the gospel merely models a moral vision, and Christianity provides only one of many ways to God. Without the virgin birth, salvation history has no savior.

The truthfulness of the virgin birth, therefore, creates a moral obligation. In other words, because Scripture affirms the virgin birth, then it is true; and if it is true, then it must be believed. To deny the virgin birth, despite the fact that the Gospels assert it, would compromise the authority of Scripture. Liberal theologians can either embrace or deny the truthfulness of the virgin birth, but both choices have significance for the entirety of Scripture. Christians, however, do not have a choice to accept or reject the truth of Scripture. Scripture exercises authority over the Christian, and he or she must accept its truth.

To believers the virgin birth has even more substance. The one who was conceived of the Holy Spirit in the virgin's womb was also conceived by the Holy Spirit in the hearts of Christians. Through the miracle of the gospel—which starts at the virgin birth—God brings forth new life from a thoroughly sinful people. Do not be embarrassed by the virgin birth; rather, teach it, preach it, and share it as a part of the gospel story so that when a person responds in faith, they will know in whom they believe. Pray to see the miracle of Christ conceived in their hearts the way he was conceived in Mary's womb. The child in Bethlehem's manger was the child whose heel would smite the serpent and in whose name Christians gather.

SUFFERED UNDER PONTIUS PILATE

Mel Gibson's film *The Passion of the Christ* hit the box office with a bang in 2004. At that time the movie generated a great deal of controversy. Disagreement also abounded about the propriety of portraying Jesus through the medium of cinematography.

All this controversy piqued the interest of prospective viewers, and as a result, the film performed well at the box office. In fact, it went on to become one of the most discussed cultural products of the era. Before the movie officially released, I was invited to a special screening of the film. I had, however, reservations about attending. On the one hand I had a deep conviction that no artistic representation could capture the infinite depths of the person of Christ and that a cinematic presentation of our Lord's crucifixion would flatten out the supernatural aspects of the work of Christ on the cross. On the other hand I felt duty-bound to speak about the movie in an informed way, and that required going to see the movie myself. Ultimately, I decided to go to the screening with my theological reservations in tow.

As I entered the theater, the size of the crowd surprised me. With every seat taken the room buzzed with conversation. The viewers seemed ready to dissect the movie and pick it apart in order to analyze its artistic presentation, its cinematography, its directing, and all the rest. My skepticism about the film seemed validated already. For them this movie amounted to just another Hollywood production. Once the film started, the clamoring voices faded into silence. The narrative of the film rushed toward the conclusion, the passion—or crucifixion—of our Lord. The violence, prolonged and escalated through so much of the film, jarred the senses. Ironically, in the midst of it all, the audience, while glued to the screen, was nonchalantly shoveling popcorn into their mouths. How, I thought, could a person watch such a scene, the depiction of the crucifixion of the Son of God, and eat popcorn?

Then I realized that they did not understand the gravity of this historical event. Even the people who put Jesus to death failed to grasp the significance of what they did because "if they had, they would not have crucified the Lord of glory" (1 Cor. 2:8). For those whose eyes the Spirit of God has not opened, the death of Jesus amounts to nothing less than a brute fact of history. For those, however, who have placed their faith in Christ and experienced the power of the resurrection, the death of Jesus stands as a paradox—at the same time the most tragic and the most glorious truth imaginable. For a Christian believer,

Jesus came as the Servant who suffered and died in our place for our sins. The Apostles' Creed enshrines this truth in its affirmation that Jesus "suffered under Pontius Pilate."

This phrase, however, seems to some a strange affirmation to include in this venerable creed for the church. Each segment of the Apostles' Creed contains an essential truth of the faith and of the gospel itself. Remove any statement from the creed's affirmations, and the whole of Christianity tumbles. Yet how could affirming that Jesus suffered under Pontius Pilate amount to a fundamental truth upon which the church must stand? What is essential about the suffering of Christ?

Substitutionary Suffering

Believers in the Lord Jesus Christ have confessed those words together across continents and across millennia *because* of the centrality of Christ's suffering to the gospel. And yet, evangelicals tend to focus almost exclusively on the substitutionary *death* of Christ. The death of Christ is one of two central and essential dimensions to the work of Christ for our salvation. The cross and the empty tomb represent these two dimensions clearly. The apostle Paul told the church at Corinth that the death of Christ on the cross *for our sins* was of first priority in the gospel of Christ along with his resurrection from the dead (1 Cor. 15:1–3).

Indeed, the apostle Paul instructed Christians to "boast" in the cross of Christ (Gal. 6:14). Christians, however, sometimes forget that Jesus did not merely *die* for us; he also *suffered* for us. Indeed, Isaiah 52–53 prophesied the *suffering* Servant who would come and rescue God's people. The text reveals the integral connection between the One who will reign disclosed as the One who will suffer. Only one person fits the description of the suffering Servant prophesied in Isaiah. His name is Jesus of Nazareth, Jesus Christ the Lord.

In Isaiah 52–53 the prophet reveals five key components of the suffering Servant. First, Isaiah discloses the promise of God that founds and secures the Servant's ministry. Next, the text reveals the mission of the Servant. Third, Isaiah demonstrates the innocence of the Servant though he suffers as one guilty. Fourth, the prophet reveals the extent of the sacrifice of the Servant. Finally, God validates the way of the cross, in that through the Servant's suffering comes vindication.

The Promise

The prophecy on the suffering Servant begins with a promise in Isaiah 52:13 (NASB): "Behold, My servant will prosper." The entire mission of the suffering Servant begins with a promise direct from God himself. Because of God's promise, the work of the suffering Servant will accomplish its purpose. It cannot fail. In Isaiah 52–53 God does not present a tentative proposal for his people. He thunders forth from the courts of heaven a promise for his covenant people. He promises a Servant who will save, and he promises the prosperity of his Servant's work.

This news from the prophet's lips would have encouraged his listeners. Though Israel found itself under God's judgment and the scorn of its enemies, God promised them a Servant who will prosper and be vindicated. Christians, however, recognize the fullness of this promise that culminated in the work of Jesus. As such, the affirmation of "suffered under Pontius Pilate" finds its very roots in the promise of Isaiah 52:13. Christians know the realization of the promise of God through Jesus' suffering.

Though he suffered on the cross and endured the wrath of God for his people, God's promise stood fulfilled on that day of Jesus' death. The prosperity of his Servant came through his suffering as he atoned for the people of God with his very blood. The life and ministry of Jesus prospered as it ended with God's glorious victory over the grave on the cross of Christ. Jesus fulfilled the promise as he hung on that tree.

The Mission

"Suffered under Pontius Pilate" enshrines the mission of Jesus' incarnation. Isaiah 53:4–6 details that mission:

> Surely he has borne our griefs and carried our sorrows; yet we esteemed him stricken, smitten by God, and afflicted. But he was pierced for our transgressions; he was crushed for our iniquities; upon him was the chastisement that brought us peace, and with his wounds we are healed.

The suffering Servant comes to bear grief, carry sorrows, and stand afflicted among man and God. The intentionality of the suffering resounds from the words, "pierced *for* our transgressions . . . crushed *for* our iniquities . . . *with* his wounds we are healed." This is the cadence of the Servant's life as he marched toward a substitutionary suffering whereby he took the transgressions of God's people on himself.

The early Christians demonstrated an incalculable sense of wisdom and gospel fidelity by including Jesus' suffering under Pilate in the Apostles' Creed. Their insight was deeply biblical. The mission of Jesus' life pointed to the cross. His incarnation took place so that he might hang on the cross and suffer on his path there. The joy of Christmas occurs only for the scandal of the cross. Paul proclaimed, "For our sake he made him to be sin who knew no sin, so that in him we might become the righteousness of God" (2 Cor. 5:21). This verse encapsulates the mission of the suffering Servant. He came *for* our sake. He came *to take* our sin. He came *to live* a sinless life. He came *to make* his people righteous. This he did through his substitutionary suffering. His suffering for his people points to the very purpose of his incarnation.

His Innocence

The innocence of the suffering Servant remains central to Isaiah's prophecy and the entirety of the gospel message. Isaiah wrote, "He was oppressed, and he was afflicted, yet he opened not his mouth; like a lamb that is led to the slaughter, and like a sheep that before its shearers is silent, so he opened not his mouth" (53:7). Jesus embodied Isaiah's prophecy as he stood silent before his accusers, willingly handing himself over to the slaughter. The Jewish authorities called for his crucifixion, though he had lived a sinless, perfect life.

Jesus encompassed all the hopes and expectations of the Old Testament. The Messiah stood in the presence of the people of Israel, and they called for his execution. When given the chance to release Jesus or the murderer Barabbas, the crowds wanted Barabbas. Pilate, only with the derived authority granted him by God, handed Jesus over to the pangs of the cross. Throughout this horrific episode Jesus, the perfect Son of God, who could have called down a legion of angels, remained silent. He came to die as the spotless, silent lamb, allowing hands that he had spoken into existence to crucify him on a sinner's cross.

The suffering Servant of God committed no crime and upheld the law with perfect obedience. The Servant "had done no violence, and there was no deceit in his mouth" (Isa. 53:9). This innocence, however, remains crucial to the gospel and to the confession of the Apostles' Creed. The Servant's innocence endowed his sacrifice with its perfect cleansing power for sin. Jesus' innocence ensured his status as a *spotless* lamb who could atone for the sins of all God's people for all eternity. His innocence accomplished the effectual power of the gospel's ability to save sinners. There would be no power in the gospel if not for the perfect life and total innocence of Jesus as he stood before the slaughter.

His Sacrifice

Isaiah's prophecy concerning the sacrifice of the Servant should jar the senses. The language he used reveals the intensity and depth of the Servant's suffering. Isaiah wrote, "Yet it was the will of the LORD to crush him; he has put him to grief" (53:10). God purposed to *crush* the Servant. He actively *willed* the death of his Anointed. This God did for the sake of his people. The culmination of this prophecy came through the Father who willed to crush his eternal Son.

None should pass over this truth without serious contemplation of its gravity and weight. The Son did not devise his own plan for salvation. He came to do the will of his Father. Jesus knew every step of his ministry moved him closer to the work his Father sent him to do: to pay for the sins of his people through his sacrifice. The Father sent the Son. The Son willingly came. Jesus lived a life of obedience to the point of death, even death on a cross (Phil. 2:8).

The author of Hebrews reflected on the nature of Jesus' sacrifice and its superiority to the old covenant: "But when Christ appeared as a high priest of the good things that have come, then through the greater and more perfect tent . . . he entered once for all into the holy places, not by means of the blood of goats and calves but by means of his own blood, thus securing an eternal redemption" (9:11–12).

Jesus entered the place of atonement himself. He entered dressed in the garments of the high priest to do the work of atoning for the sins of the people. Then, in a shocking turn of events, he removed his priestly garments and sacrificed himself on the altar. He brought no goat or sheep to sacrifice. That system had not accomplished a final and lasting redemption. He entered the heavenly tabernacle himself to lay himself down upon the altar as the perfect and *last* sacrifice for the sins of the people. He shed his blood and poured himself out. The crimson flow and scarlet tide of his suffering and crucifixion made propitiation for our sins forever. This sacrifice existed as a shadow in Isaiah's prophecy as he declared the will of God to crush the Servant. That prophecy came to fruition as the Son went to the altar and as his Father crushed him in our place.

The Vindication

Finally, the immeasurable sufferings of the Servant culminate in his promised vindication.

> Out of the anguish of his soul he shall see and be satisfied;
> by his knowledge shall the righteous one, my servant,
> make many to be accounted righteous,
> and he shall bear their iniquities.
> Therefore I will divide him a portion with the many,
> and he shall divide the spoil with the strong,
> because he poured out his soul to death
> and was numbered with the transgressors;
> yet he bore the sin of many,
> and makes intercession for the transgressors. (Isa. 53:11–12)

Isaiah reveals the purpose of the suffering and displays in resplendent glory what the Servant accomplished through his agony. Jesus' suffering bore the iniquities of the people. In so doing Jesus *satisfied* God's wrath against sin. Jesus *satisfied* God's judgment. Jesus *satisfied* God's holiness. All the longings of redemptive history, all the groans of the creation subjected to sin find their rest and hope in the sufferings of Jesus Christ. He paid it all. He secured it all. Nothing else need be done. *It was finished.*

Isaiah's prophecy points to the vindication of the Son through his accomplished work. Jesus' sufferings accomplish justification as he makes "many to be accounted righteous" (Isa. 53:11). As he bore the sins of many, he secured eternal salvation for the people of God. His sufferings, though scandalous and horrific, changed the world. His sufferings altered the course of eternity for countless souls who, without his sacrifice, marched toward perennial perdition.

Christians, therefore, must grasp the glory of Christ's sufferings. As the words of Isaiah come to their fruition in the person and work of Christ, the necessity of "suffered under Pontius Pilate" shines all the brighter; not as a mere historical affirmation but a pillar of gospel truth. Isaiah reveals that through the suffering of the Servant, God will vindicate his name and his people. Indeed, through suffering comes glory. Through the excruciating sufferings of Jesus, God accomplished atonement for his people.

What, Therefore, Did the Christ Suffer?

The affirmation "suffered under Pontius Pilate" enshrines the prophetic pronouncement of Isaiah 52–53 and the fulfillment detailed in the sufferings of Jesus Christ. The creed affirms the reality of the historicity of the event by including the name "Pontius Pilate." The suffering of Jesus constitutes an actual historical event that occurred in a certain place and time as revealed in Scripture. The creed, however, affirms much more than mere historicity in affirming the suffering of Jesus under Pilate. It captures a vital component of Jesus' ministry, without which the gospel would be emptied of its power. The creed highlights the significance of Christ's suffering. What, therefore, did the Christ suffer?

Bodily Suffering

Contemporary Christians often fail to consider the physical sufferings of Jesus. Perhaps, cautious Christians find themselves unwilling to broach the topic because of the quagmire of christology. Christians have difficulty in thinking about the reality of the two natures in the one person of Jesus Christ—namely, his humanity and his divinity. The difficulty of this doctrine for our fallen, fallible minds, however, must not inhibit Christians from the clear teachings of the Scriptures. The Bible allows Christians to think of the God-man as suffering in his body.

Jesus suffered many things physically. The Bible reveals his suffering in the following ways:

- Jesus experienced hunger. (Mark 11:12)
- Jesus experienced thirst. (John 4:7)
- Jesus felt weariness. (John 4:6)
- Jesus needed to sleep. (Mark 4:38)

The Bible clearly teaches the humanity of Jesus through the things he and all humans suffer. The reality that the God-man experienced suffering should, therefore, influence our reading of the sufferings described in Jesus' trial, flogging, and crucifixion.

Jesus, the eternal Son of God, experienced the fullness of pain that would have accompanied his torture and execution. The Roman methods of flogging would dispense maximum pain to the victim while keeping them from death or shock. The methods of the torture intended the victim to feel and experience every ounce of pain rendered. Jesus, the Son of God, fully man, experienced every bit of pain through the suffering of his torture and crucifixion.

That Jesus experienced suffering as fully human only magnifies the glory of his intentionality and obedience to suffer and fulfill the prophecy of Isaiah. The Son of God willingly placed himself into the intense, horrific, and excruciating pain of Roman torture and crucifixion. This he did for his people. His sufferings demonstrate the infinite love of God in Christ for his people in our place. He endured the pain, contempt, reviling, and his very flesh ripped from his body out of divine love for a rebellious, sinful people.

Spiritual Suffering

In addition to the physical suffering that Jesus endured for God's people, he also suffered as a curse under the wrath of God in our place. This he did in order to accomplish redemption, propitiation, and the forgiveness of sin. In short, he endured the wrath of God to purchase the good news of the gospel.

Paul wrote, "Christ redeemed us from the curse of the law by becoming a curse for us—for it is written, 'Cursed is everyone who is hanged on a tree'" (Gal. 3:13). Paul magnifies the sufferings of Christ as he reveals the redemptive function Jesus played while he hung on the cross. Not only did Christ suffer bodily, he suffered as a curse. All God's people had sinned and fallen short of the glory of God (Rom. 3:23). Everyone lived under the curse of the law, for none had kept the law. Jesus, however, became the curse. He took on himself the wrath of God against sin.

In becoming the curse Jesus experienced the fullness of God's wrath and judgment for the sin of mankind. God poured on Christ the eternal punishment due for each and every sin committed by his people. Jesus endured it all, suffered it all, took it all upon himself. For the several hours he hung on the cross, Jesus suffered the eternal punishment of a sinner, thus satisfying God's wrath. "Since, therefore, we have now been justified by his blood, much more shall we be saved by him from the wrath of God" (Rom. 5:9). Paul proclaimed the splendid riches and accomplishment of Christ's sufferings on the cross. By his blood, he satisfied the wrath of God. Through his suffering he accomplished salvation. He, furthermore, endured the punishment for sin who all deserve *yet none who have faith in him will ever experience.*

Respond to His Suffering

That last sentence contains impeccable and eternally precious glory. All God's people deserve for eternity what Christ took in our place. Yet none who have faith in him will ever experience the punishment and fury of God's wrath because Christ satisfied the justice of God. Christ suffered so that we who have faith in him will never endure the fires of hell. The sufferings of Christ, therefore, call each and every one of us to respond.

Believe in the Promise of God

The sufferings of Christ stand as a monolith, reminding all that God keeps his word and promises. Jesus' suffering, therefore, should cause all God's people to trust in God at all times. He has displayed his love for his people. He has demonstrated the infinitude of his love. Paul wrote, "He who did not spare his own Son but gave him up for us all, how will he not also with him graciously give us all things?" (Rom. 8:32). God willed the crushing of his Son as a demonstration of his love for us that he might satisfy his wrath against our sin. God's love flows down the blood-stained cross of Jesus Christ. God did not withhold even his Son to save his people. The sufferings of Christ, therefore, beckon God's people to believe in him, trust in him, and hold fast to his promises.

Join in Christ's Sufferings

The sufferings of Christ purchased for Christians a new heart and an indwelling power through the ministry of the Holy Spirit (Rom. 8:14–17). As such, the Bible commissions God's people to follow in the footsteps of their Savior, to take up their cross and follow him. The apostle Paul viewed the call to suffering not as a burden but a glorious joy to receive. In Philippians 3:7–11 Paul demonstrated two glorious truths in imitating the suffering of Christ.

Suffering for a Surpassing Worth

Paul wrote, "Indeed, I count everything as loss because of the surpassing worth of knowing Christ Jesus my Lord. For his sake I have suffered the loss of all things and count them as rubbish" (v. 8). Paul recognized the reality of suffering for a Christian. Christians will suffer in this life in many different ways. In Philippians 3 Paul had in mind the suffering endured as Christians cast off the lures, enticements, and pleasure of a lost and dying world. Christians suffer the loss of all the temporal world can offer in order to gain something surpassing in worth. Paul suffered the loss of the world to gain Christ. Knowledge of Christ possesses a worth far beyond anything the world can offer. Thus, he willingly suffered the loss of all the world can promise in order to know Jesus Christ. In this way Christians, too, must suffer the loss of the world if we want to gain a relationship with Jesus.

Share His Sufferings and Death for the Resurrection to Come

Paul exclaimed his willingness to suffer as a Christian. His words in Philippians 3 assault and offend the convenience and comfort-driven confines of Western Christianity. Paul's insight, however, must resound as the heartbeat of every Christian and pulse through the veins of those claiming the name of Jesus Christ. Paul wrote about the reason why he was willing to lose everything: "That I may know him and the power of his resurrection, *and may share his sufferings, becoming like him in his death*, that by any means possible I may attain the resurrection from the dead" (vv. 10–11). Paul longed to share in the sufferings of Christ and to imitate him in his death. Why? Paul did not think he could serve as another atoning sacrifice for sins. Paul did not think he could replace the work of Jesus Christ. Paul's desire to follow in Christ's sufferings, however, stemmed from his passion for the gospel as the only hope of salvation to a lost world condemned to an eternity in hell.

Paul desired to imitate his Savior because he knew the way of glory comes through the way of the cross. The economy of God dispenses with the worldly inclinations and wisdom of the Stoics. God established a wisdom that glorifies the lowly and condemns the haughty. Paul took upon himself the yoke of

Christ—a yoke of suffering—because *it is worth it*. The fruit of Christian suffering culminates in a resurrection. Christian suffering ends with a new, eternal body secured by the sufferings of Jesus Christ.

Conclusion

The Christian hymnody of Isaac Watts proclaims the excellencies of Paul's words in Philippians 3 and the suffering of Christ proclaimed in the Apostles' Creed. Watts wrote:

> When I survey the wondrous Cross,
> On which the prince of glory died,
> My richest gain I count but loss,
> And pour contempt on all my pride.

> Forbid it Lord that I should boast
> Save in the death of Christ my God;
> All the vain things that charm me most,
> I sacrifice them to His blood.

> See from his head, his hands, his feet,
> Sorrow and love flow mingled down;
> Did e're such love and sorrow meet,
> or thorns compose so rich a crown?

> His dying crimson like a robe,
> Spreads o'er his body on the tree;
> Then am I dead to all the globe,
> And all the globe is dead to me.

Were the whole realm of nature mine,
That were a present far too small;
Love so amazing, love so divine,
Demands my soul, my life, my all.[1]

This glorious Christian hymn contains vivid imagery of Christ's cross and the sufferings he endured at Golgotha. Unlike the popcorn munching I witnessed during the *Passion of the Christ*, Watts's hymn makes us look at the cross and the sufferings of Jesus and worship. Jesus' sufferings on the cross secured our eternal life with God. No crown of earthly kings can compare to the crown of thorns pressed into the brow of Jesus. No throne can resemble the resplendent wonder of Christ's cross.

The last two stanzas of Watts's hymn reflect on the crimson flow of Jesus' sufferings and its implications for the church. Through Jesus' suffering Christians are to die to the world and find life in Christ. The splendid display of scandalous love on the cross beckons God's people to lay down their lives for the surpassing worth of knowing Christ. Jesus' sufferings accomplished our salvation, justification, and eternal life; and they summon the church to glory in his sacrifice and follow in his steps. Indeed, Christ suffered under Pontius Pilate, and thus, we are saved.

CHAPTER SIX

WAS CRUCIFIED, DEAD, AND BURIED

As a young man, I encountered a New Testament scholar who had many strong feelings about the cross of Christ. He absolutely hated the idea that the crucifixion of Christ was necessary for our salvation. He hated the very idea of Christ's death as our substitute, paying the penalty for our sins that we ourselves could not pay. He heartily rejected what he called "bloody cross religion"—the message of the cross.

But, the Bible reveals so clearly that Christ died *for our* sins and that the payment for the penalty for our sins was necessary. As the apostle Paul teaches us, the cross, and the cross alone, reveals how God can be both "just and the justifier of the one who has faith in Jesus" (Rom. 3:26). Indeed, the unmistakable symbol of Christianity is a cross. The fact that a horrifying instrument of execution in the Roman Empire has been turned into a symbol of love, beauty, and devotion requires an explanation.

That explanation is called the New Testament. The message of the cross is the good news of salvation, and the story of the cross is the story of God's love for sinners. The most amazing truth is that God loves sinners and Christ died for the ungodly. As the apostle Paul wrote, "God shows his love for us in that while were still sinners, Christ died for us" (Rom. 5:8). The apostle John instructed Christians to reflect on "what kind of love the Father has given to us" in the salvation that took place on the cross, so that those who are Christ's people "should be called children of God" (1 John 3:1).

The Apostles' Creed takes us to the central truths of our salvation when we confess that Jesus Christ, God's only Son, "was crucified, dead, and buried." These three words, *crucified*, *dead*, and *buried* tell the story of the cross in its power and in its brutal force.

The three central truths confirmed here affirm the fact that Jesus was crucified on a cross by the act of scornful men, that he truly died, and that after his death he was buried—all of this in perfect fulfillment of the plan of God.

When the apostle Peter preached on the day of Pentecost, he told the massive crowd assembled before him: "Men of Israel, hear these words: Jesus of Nazareth, a man attested to you by God with mighty works and wonders and signs that God did through him in your midst, as you yourselves know—this Jesus, delivered up according to the definite plan and foreknowledge of God, you crucified and killed by the hands of lawless men" (Acts 2:22–23). This text underlines that the cross was not something that surprised God or merely happened to Jesus. It was God's plan.

When John the Baptist saw Jesus, he cried out, "Behold, the Lamb of God, who takes away the sin of the world" (John 1:29). The lamb, spotless and without blemish, was the best-known symbol of the entire system of blood sacrifice.

Jesus told his disciples: "Greater love has no one than this, that someone lay down his life for his friends" (John 15:13). Speaking of his life, Jesus made clear that he would go to the cross willingly: "No one takes it from me, but I lay it down of my own accord. I have authority to lay it down, and I have authority to take it up again. This charge I have received from my Father" (John 10:18).

This is why Christians look to Jesus on the cross as a victor, not a victim. He came for this purpose, and he fulfilled this redeeming purpose—completely.

The centrality of the cross to the Christian life, however, has enemies. Some are repelled by the very idea of the cross, the concept of blood atonement, and the necessity of Christ's death for sin. Indeed, those who levy such complaints believe the scandal of the cross has no place in the modern and progressive world. As we look more closely at the depths of the cross, we need to look at some of these objections. If Christians let this phrase in the Apostles' Creed crumble beneath the weight of heterodoxy, they forfeit their salvation, surrender their hope, and miss the glories of God displayed in the scandal of Calvary.

The Enemies of the Cross

The modern enemies of the cross of Christ have their roots in the times of the apostles. Paul wrote, "For many, of whom I have often told you and now tell you even with tears, *walk as enemies of the cross of Christ*" (Phil. 3:18). The message of the cross offends prideful and darkened minds. The cross requires an acknowledgment of sin and the impossibility of any works-based salvation.

Obviously, opponents come from the secular world and from those of other faiths. The most dangerous detractors, however, originate from within the ranks of confused Christians. These critics of the cross espouse false teachings that, if left unanswered, can lead many away from the truth. In their attack on Christ's cross, they lay three charges against historical and biblical Christianity. First, they deny the necessity of a sacrifice for sin. Second, they reject the cross because it would represent a case of divine child abuse. Finally, some opponents deny the historicity of the cross narratives and ascribe only moral lessons to those texts.

The Repugnance of Sacrifice

I had a seminary professor who detested the thought that a death had to take place in order for God to forgive sin. The heart of this objection flows from an aversion to the sacrificial system—an aversion that sees bloodshed and sacrifice as nothing more than cold murder and unnecessary loss of life. A God who would require such a system for forgiveness has no place in the modern system of justice that humanity has attained. A God of love and grace does not need to atone for sin through the shedding of blood. Of course such beliefs also reveal a horrible misunderstanding of the holiness of God and the reality of sin. If you can imagine the holiness of God and rob him of this most important attribute, you can also redefine sin as something less than an infinite violation of God's holiness.

The Bible, however, could not affirm substitutionary atonement any more clearly. The author of Hebrews wrote, "Without the shedding of blood there is no forgiveness of sins" (9:22). The

Bible's understanding of the seriousness of sin and the holiness of God go hand in hand. The proponents of this objection find the need for a sacrifice repugnant because they do not understand sin as repugnant, an infinite rebellion against a holy God and a violation of his holy law. My old seminary professor could not comprehend a god who would require a sacrifice for sin, because he had created a god of his own imagination—very different from the God of holy Scripture. The god he crafted fell infinitely short of the glory and holiness that God reveals of himself in the Scriptures.

The Bible answers this objection in two ways. First, it reveals the glory of God in his holiness:

And you shall not profane my holy name, that I may be sanctified among the people of Israel. I am the LORD who sanctifies you. (Lev. 22:32)

> There is none holy like the LORD:
> for there is none besides you;
> there is no rock like our God. (1 Sam. 2:2)

> God reigns over the nations;
> God sits on his holy throne. (Ps. 47:8)

> "Holy, holy, holy is the LORD of hosts;
> the whole earth is full of his glory!" (Isa. 6:3)

> "You shall be holy, for I am holy." (1 Peter 1:16)

Each of these texts reveal the resplendent beauty of God and the purity of his holiness. His name, throne, rule—indeed, his very essence—exude a glorious holiness that distinguishes God from all the creation. God reigns as the Creator who created *ex nihilo*, out of nothing. Nothing in all creation compares to him. The very essence of God, therefore, detests sin and must dispose of any rebellion against his holy and righteous rule.

Second, the Bible corrects these detractors by showing the seriousness of sin and its consequences:

> But transgressors shall be altogether destroyed;
> the future of the wicked shall be cut off. (Ps. 37:38)

> I will punish the world for its evil,
> and the wicked for their iniquity;
> I will put an end to the pomp of the arrogant,
> and lay low the pompous pride of the ruthless. (Isa. 13:11)

> For behold, the LORD is coming out from his place
> to punish the inhabitants of the earth for their iniquity.
> (Isa. 26:21)

> For all who have sinned without the law will also perish without the law, and all who have sinned under the law will be judged by the law. (Rom. 2:12)

> For the wages of sin is death. (Rom. 6:23)

The holiness of God bubbles over into his wrath against sin. God must punish sin; for, nothing in all the cosmos equates to greater evil than the sinfulness of mankind. Sin represents an open declaration of war against the rule and authority of God. The wages of such sin will be a swift and eternal death.

Our God, however, did not leave humanity without hope. He provided a way of forgiveness. In the Old Testament he provided the sacrificial system. God, by his grace, placed his wrath upon the sacrifice. The priest atoned for the sins of the people through the sacrificial offering. This system, however, could never make full atonement for sin. God, therefore, in a display of scandalous grace, sent his only Son to be the once-and-for-all sacrifice for sin. His precious blood eternally atones for the sins of God's people. Without his sacrifice all would still live in sin and without hope. To deny, therefore, the need of a sacrifice, amounts to nothing less than a denial of the gospel.

God the Cosmic Child Abuser

Others deny the necessity of Christ's death because they claim it would promote an act of divine child abuse by God the Father. These opponents ask, "Who can love a God who kills his own Son?" They shudder at the thought of a Father who abandons his Son to the cross of a criminal. Anyone who subscribes to the biblical concept of the sacrifice of Christ, therefore, promotes a perverse God who abandoned his Son to fierce persecution and then endured the fullness of God's wrath against sin.

This position, however, insulates the crucifixion narrative from the rest of biblical revelation. First, the Bible often describes the love that exists between the Son and the Father. At Jesus' baptism the Father expresses the deep love and pleasure he possesses for Christ (Matt. 3:17). Paul pronounced the glory the Father bestowed upon Christ *because* of his obedience and sacrifice (Phil. 2:9–11). The Father *exalts* his Son above all creation. Through Jesus' sacrifice the Father bestowed upon him a name above every name that will prostrate all creation.

Second, Jesus made clear that he hung on the cross not by

abandonment but by his own will and desire. Jesus said, "I am the good shepherd. The good shepherd lays down his life for the sheep" (John 10:11). The author of Hebrews tells us that for the joy set before Jesus, he endured the cross (12:2). The Bible does not speak of a Father abandoning a child to the cross. It describes, rather, a Son who willingly gave up his life for his people. *He* laid down his life for his sheep. *He* set his face toward the cross, endured its shame, obeyed the will of his Father, and accomplished salvation for all God's people.

The Cross—Only a Moral Lesson?

In our current culture the cross is used to decorate our homes and drape around our necks as jewelry. Some use the cross as a symbol of moral and ethical teaching—a call to serve our fellow man. These manifestations divorce the cross from its true meaning—the place where God poured out his wrath on his Son to forgive our sin. The Scriptures clearly detail that when God created the world, he purposed his Son to redeem sinners by the shedding of his blood (Eph. 1:3–10).

Unfortunately, sentimentality and emotionalism invade the ranks of Christianity. This gospel of sentimentality preaches that the cross merely transforms us by example into more loving creatures. This false gospel upholds Jesus' love on the cross as an ethic for all to imitate rather than an event necessary for salvation. Thus, the cross did not accomplish atonement. Rather, the cross merely pictured a kind of suffering love that ought to cause us to change our disposition toward God and others. This theology assumes a lack of a sin problem in the creation. The cross, in this heterodox theology, serves as God's attempt at good public relations where he displays love as a coaxing mechanism to draw humanity into trusting him.

The cross, however, did not solve a divine public relations problem. It satisfied the burning wrath of God against our sin. The cross, no doubt, demonstrated God's love. His love, however, shines infinitely brighter when viewed through the paradigm of sin. As we have seen, Romans 5:8 says, "But God shows his love for us in that while we were still sinners, Christ died for us." Those who would make the cross a mere ethical lesson and public relations event of God's love empty the cross of all its loving effect. The cross thundered forth the love of God in spectacular power as God sacrificed his own Son in place of us. God poured his wrath upon his Son, executing justice for our rebellion against him. At the same time he placed upon sinners the perfect righteousness of Jesus Christ. He credited our sin to Christ and gave us his righteousness through faith. This is true love. This is scandalous love. This is glorious love that calls us to worship.

A Final Word Against the Detractors

The Bible presents Christ as the holy sacrifice that atones for the sins of those who believe. The gospel, therefore, proclaims much more than an attractive sentimental message. It contains the very power of God for salvation as it beckons sinners to place their faith and trust in the sacrificial work of Jesus Christ.

Though denied by some, the atoning work on the cross reveals the fullness of God's nature and character. In the crucifixion, humanity observes the depth of God's hatred toward sin. In Christ's death God's people view the tragic consequences of our rebellion. In the cross God's people also learn the depth of God's love. He does not leave his people in their sin, damned to an eternity in hell. He comes to rescue them from the grip of Satan by delivering his own Son. In the cross God acted out of his perfect nature and character. Thus, God revealed in Jesus' sacrifice the overwhelming intersection of his divine love and justice.

The Scriptures also attest to the necessity of the cross. Paul, in Romans 3:21 and following, pointed to the cross as the place where God the Father set forth his Son out of love for humanity as a "propitiation" for sin. This constituted a demonstration of God's own righteousness. This logic reveals how God, in his holiness, must require a sacrifice for sin and at the same time do it out of his love. John Stott commented on the relationship between God's love and justice:

> We must never think of this duality with God's being as irreconcilable. For God is not at odds with himself, however much it may appear to us that he is. He is "the God of peace," of inner tranquility, not turmoil. True, we find it difficult to hold in our minds simultanously the images of God as the Judge who must punish evil-doers and of the Lover who must find a way to forgive them. Yet, he is both, and at the same time.[1]

Paul also clearly knew that man cannot pay the penalty of sin. Only the sinless God could pay the price and penalty for sin. Only the perfect obedience of the spotless Lamb could provide the blood that pays the eternal price for sin. As Paul commented in Philippians 2, Jesus humbled himself "even [to] death on a cross" so that those who come to Christ might experience justification. In the sacrifice of Jesus, God the Father revealed both his justice in requiring a sacrifice for sin and his role as the justifier by providing the sacrifice in Christ.

To deny substitutionary atonement, one denies the nature of

God and the only hope of salvation for mankind. Furthermore, to deny the atoning work of Christ nullifies Christ's mission on earth. In 1909 Scottish theologian P. T. Forsyth wrote a book entitled *The Cruciality of the Cross*. In it he underlined the integral relationship between Christ and the cross:

> Christ is to us just what his cross is. All that Christ was in heaven or on Earth was put into what he did there. . . . Christ I repeat is to us just what his cross is. You do not understand Christ till you understand his cross.[2]

Forsyth's words call all believers to that old rugged cross. He admonished us to never let go of its power and revelation. Without the cross salvation never happened. Without the cross mankind remains blinded by sin. Without the cross none can know God.

The Cross: The Symbol of Our Faith

The necessity of the cross for the Christian life has spanned the ages of the church. Indeed, the early church fathers and leaders could have adopted many different signs and symbols as an emblem of the Christian faith. Nothing, however, could eclipse the meaning and glory of the cross. Jesus' cross represents a powerful symbol for the faith because of its centrality, scandalousness, and glory.

Centrality

Paul wrote, "For I delivered to you as of *first importance* what I also received: that Christ died for our sins in accordance with the Scriptures, that he was buried, that he was raised on the third day in accordance with the Scriptures" (1 Cor. 15:3–4). Paul reminded the Corinthians of the centrality of the cross. He proclaimed the primary and central importance of the death of Christ for the forgiveness of sin. Paul cannot comprehend his ministry and gospel without the cross of Jesus Christ. The apostles, therefore, erected the cross as a central pillar of truth in the earliest days of the church.

Scandalousness

The enemies of Christianity pressed the cross upon early Christians as a form of persecution. They sought to humiliate Christians so that the wider culture might reject them. Christians, however, were not *embarrassed* by the cross. Instead they *embraced* it. Paul wrote, "But we preach Christ crucified: a stumbling block to Jews and foolishness to Gentiles" (1 Cor. 1:23 NIV). The cross, in Roman times, represented the pinnacle of suffering and helplessness. The cross punished criminals or people in opposition to the government. To preach the cross, therefore, amounted to grave foolishness. The cross, however, stands as the altar of an eternal sacrifice for sin.

Jesus' death on the cross defeated death, broke the chains of Satan, and set the captive free. The cross of Christ ascends as a monolith of salvation where God's love and justice meet together in beautiful, scandalous power. The church clung to the cross precisely because of its scandalous beauty. There on that Roman cross, God accomplished salvation in Christ. Though a stumbling block to some and foolishness to the world, the power of God for salvation flows from the crimson tide of Christ's blood on Calvary's cross.

Glory

Paul wrote, "But far be it from me to boast except in the cross of our Lord Jesus Christ, by which the world has been crucified to me, and I to the world" (Gal. 6:14). Paul confessed that his life amounted to nothing apart from the cross of Jesus Christ. Paul exclaimed the glory of losing the world for the sake of gaining Christ (Phil. 3:7–8). The cross meant everything to Paul. Without the cross he had no life, no ministry, no hope, no joy.

The cross, therefore, enshrines the true glory of every believer in Jesus Christ. The cross stands not as a tool of execution but as a monument of glory. The cross empties the world of its passing beauty and offers an eternal life with God himself. Through the cross condemnation ends (Rom. 8:1). Through the cross we can partake in redemption (Eph. 1:7). Through the cross God lavishly blesses his people with every blessing of the heavenly realm (Eph. 1:4, 7–8). Jesus on the cross contains a magnificent and indescribable glory that overshadows every earthly ambition and hope. The cross is our glory.

Crucified, Dead, and Buried—John 19 and the Crucifixion of Jesus

With all this in mind, the words of the creed, "crucified, dead, and buried," serve as essential pillars of the Christian truth and point to the centrality of the cross as the symbol of the Christian faith. In John 19 the historical account of Jesus' crucifixion, death, and burial take center stage. This account records many details that offer proof of the validity of Jesus' actual death and burial. More important, John's account causes readers to come face-to-face with the death of the Son of God. This captivating narrative reveals the purposes of Jesus' coming and ministry. He came to die for the sins of the world. John 19 reveals the unparalleled story of the scandalous, glorious, and history-altering sacrifice of Jesus Christ.

The Rejection of Jesus

The story does not begin with Jesus, suddenly, hanging on a cross. Something devastating occurred for this sinless Savior and Messiah to end up on a criminal's cross. John recorded,

> Now it was the day of Preparation of the Passover. It was about the sixth hour. He [Pilate] said to the Jews, "Behold your King!" They cried out, "Away with him, away with him, crucify him!" Pilate said to them, "Shall I crucify your King?" The chief priests answered, "We have no king but Caesar." (John 19:14–15)

In this horrific scene the people of God reject the spotless Son. The religious leaders had longed for the day when the Messiah would come. Their Scriptures ached for the coming of God's anointed one. He had, in fact, come. Jesus walked with them, healed their sick, raised the dead from the grave, cast out demons, and taught with authority. The Messiah had come, and they cried out, "Crucify him!"

Pilate, the Roman governor, tries to keep Jesus off the cross. He has found the accusations levied against Jesus lacking and baseless. In his final plea he asks the mob, "Shall I crucify your King?" The response of the leaders reveals the height of their darkened hearts and the depth of their sin. They exclaim, "We have no king but Caesar." In this very moment, the people of

God reject him as their king and espouse their allegiance to a worldly ruler. Jesus, however, remains silent. Like a sheep before the slaughter, he silently endured the rejection of a people he had brought into existence.

Jesus Crucified

The narrative now turns to that long march up Calvary to Golgotha, the place of the skull. "There they crucified him, and with him two others, one on either side, and Jesus between them" (John 19:18). The Son of glory, very God of very God, now hoisted up on a Roman cross. They exposed his body to the elements. The soldiers had flogged his body and shred his flesh to pieces. They would have done enough harm to his body to put Jesus in excruciating pain at the very threshold of sending him into shock or an early death. Now, they took nails and drove them through his wrists and his ankles. The hammer's blows pierced his flesh and painfully held him in place for others to come and mock and scorn. Yet, there he hung by his own accord, by his own will, by his own initiative. He had come to save sinners, even the ones who put him on that cross. Indeed, your sin, my sin, and the sin of all God's people held Jesus upon that cross.

Tetelestai—the Death of Jesus

The scene could not have been more devastating. All the disciples placed their hope and lives in Jesus. Hundreds and thousands in Jerusalem followed Jesus and believed in his role as the Messiah. Now, their shining hope hung on a cross and would soon perish. Jesus, however, knew how even this would end. He knew that though he hung on a cross, he continued to reign as he fulfilled every promise of the Scriptures and brought to bear the longing of all redemptive history.

After this, Jesus, knowing that all was now finished, said (to fulfill the Scripture), "I thirst." A jar full of sour wine stood there, so they put a sponge full of the sour wine on a hyssop branch and held it to his mouth. When Jesus had received the sour wine, he said, "It is finished," and he bowed his head and gave up his spirit. (John 19:28–30)

Tetelestai, "It is finished." John recorded these last words of Jesus. His final utterance shook the foundation of the earth, tore the curtain in the temple, and thundered across the sky. He had obeyed his Father's will perfectly. He set his face toward the cross and willingly offered himself up. There, on that cross, he bore the fullness of God's wrath for the sin of his people. Jesus, the Son of God, had died. No death in the history of the cosmos, however, accomplished so much. There on that cross, when Jesus uttered "*tetelestai*," he declared salvation had finally, fully, and forever come.

The Burial of Jesus

The creed affirms Jesus' crucifixion, death, *and* burial. The burial, however, remains dislodged from the place of importance in contemporary evangelical thought. Christians worship a risen, living Lord, not a dead savior. John described Jesus' burial, however, not by accident or as the conclusion of the story. Jesus' burial does not serve as a convenient placeholder between the crucifixion and the resurrection. The burial of Jesus, rather, communicates something vitally important for all that took place in his crucifixion and death.

After these things Joseph of Arimathea, who was a disciple of Jesus, but secretly for fear of the Jews, asked Pilate that he might take away the body of Jesus, and Pilate gave him permission. So he came and took away his body. Nicodemus also, who earlier had come to Jesus by night, came bringing a mixture of myrrh and aloes, about seventy-five pounds in weight. So they took the body of Jesus and bound it in linen cloths with the spices, as is the burial custom of the Jews. Now in the place where he was crucified there was a garden, and in the garden a new tomb in which no one had yet been laid. So because of the Jewish day of Preparation, since the tomb was close at hand, they laid Jesus there. (John 19:38–42)

In this text something astounding happens. Nicodemus, who had come to Jesus in John chapter 3, returns to the story. He comes to bury Jesus, not as a mere man, but as king. The myrrh and aloes he brought for Jesus' burial were employed in the burial ceremonies of kings and rulers. Nicodemus now uses them for Jesus, the *King* of kings and *Lord* of lords.

The tomb of Christ should also shock believers. The burial narrative of Christ provides a vivid illustration of the weight of Christ's atoning work. In Jesus' tomb the Son of God lay dead. The tomb, however, should not be for Jesus Christ but for his people. The tomb represents the extent of God's love and the cost of our sin. The burial of the Son of God displays the paradoxical unity of the full horror of human sin and the illustrious, cosmic, infinite, and scandalous love of God for us in Christ.

Conclusion

The words *crucified*, *dead*, and *buried* reveal the foundation of the Christian hope. The picture of a crucified King marks the symbol and message of the Christian gospel. Believers who desire to see the gospel of Jesus take root in their homes, nation, and around the world, must preach the *cross*. The Old Testament anticipated the crucifixion and prophesied its coming. Jesus understood the purpose of his time on earth. Every move he made, he did with his mind set on the cross.

Paul knew that he must preach Christ crucified and cling to that powerful gospel message. The church recognized quickly the cross as the most fitting symbol of the faith. The church fathers enshrined the cross in the Apostles' Creed for the health and vitality of the church. Today Christians must recapture again the glory of this affirmation. The words "crucified, dead, and buried" contain infinite riches of the spectacular love of God. Indeed, none can mine these words exhaustively. God's people will spend eternity marveling at his grace on the cross and will not have scratched the surface. Brothers and sisters, glory in and know the inexhaustible love of God in Christ for you in the words "crucified, dead, and buried."

CHAPTER SEVEN

HE DESCENDED INTO HELL

After Jesus died on the cross and his body was buried in the tomb, where was he? This short statement in the creed reminds us that Jesus, having truly died, was in what both the Old and New Testaments describe as the realm of the dead. The Hebrew word from the Old Testament is *sheol*, and the Greek word from the New Testament is *hades*. In both cases this refers to the temporary realm of the dead who are awaiting final judgment.

This phrase of the creed belongs here, as we shall see, but in this case, we have to be particularly careful not to go beyond what the Bible reveals about Jesus descending into hades. The brevity of this chapter is just an affirmation that we are to believe all that the Bible teaches—and resist the temptation to go further.

During the medieval era some theologians gave in to the temptation of theological speculation and went far beyond

Scripture in speaking about hell. Furthermore, the translation of *hades* into Latin and then into English can confuse us, because the word *hades* is so often translated as "hell." This is not so much wrong as it is inadequate. The New Testament Greek also includes the word *Gehenna*, which is the place of torment. The Bible does not tell us that Jesus went to *Gehenna*; what it does tell us, boldly, is that Jesus truly died. This phrase of the creed underlines that important fact.

Some Christians have wondered about 1 Peter 3:19, which speaks of Christ in the Spirit proclaiming victory to Old Testament saints such as Noah. This is completely consistent with other biblical texts such as Luke 16:19–31, which speak of the rich man who was in torment in *hades* while Lazarus, also in *hades*, was comforted in Abraham's bosom—a most honored place. *Hades*, the realm of the dead, contains both a place of torment and a place of great blessing, consistent with the entire body of holy Scripture.

Hebrews 12:2 describes Jesus Christ as "the founder and perfecter of our faith." In Hebrews 11 we are told that the saints of the Old Testament, including those celebrated in that very chapter, "though commended through their faith, did not receive what was promised, since God had provided something better for us, that apart from us they should not be made perfect" (vv. 39–40). Now, with all believers in Christ, they will be made perfect with us, and not apart from us. The very Noah mentioned in 1 Peter 3 is, of course, the same Noah honored in Hebrews 11:7. When Peter talked about "the days of Noah," he knew exactly what he meant. This same Noah, along with other heroes of the Old Testament, are commended as examples of faith. We also turn back to the Old Testament in order to understand the context of this phrase of the creed.

The psalmist wrote:

> For you will not abandon my soul to Sheol,
> or let your holy one see corruption. (Ps. 16:10)

Peter, preaching on the day of Pentecost, said that David was looking to Christ:

> Brothers, I may say to you with confidence about the patriarch David that he both died and was buried, and his tomb is with us to this day. Being therefore a prophet, and knowing that God had sworn with an oath to him that he would set one of his descendants on his throne, he foresaw and spoke about the resurrection of the Christ, that he was not abandoned to Hades, nor did his flesh see corruption. (Acts 2:29–31)

Peter said that David was not speaking of himself but of Christ. Even as Christ truly died and his body was buried in the grave, and even as his spirit entered the realm of the dead (*hades*), Christ was not abandoned nor did his body suffer corruption. Why? Because God raised him from the dead. And so, even as we confess that Christ descended into hell, we get ready to celebrate that *hades* could not hold him.

CHAPTER EIGHT

THE THIRD DAY HE AROSE AGAIN FROM THE DEAD

"Why do you seek the living among the dead?" (Luke 24:5). This is one of the most shocking questions found in the entire Bible, and it was asked by two angels, dressed in "dazzling apparel" (Luke 24:4). No one would go to a grave looking to find one who is alive, which is exactly the point the angels were making. "He is not here, but has risen," they declared (Luke 24:6).

The angels went on to remind the women who had come to the tomb to prepare the body of Jesus that, when in Galilee, the Lord had told them, "The Son of Man must be delivered into the hands of sinful men and be crucified and on the third day rise" (Luke 24:7).

Jesus Christ rose on the third day! This is the greatest good news in all of human history. The resurrection of Jesus Christ from the dead is not just a historic truth, it is not just the miracle of all miracles, it is the very promise of salvation to all who believe and repent of their sins. All of history turns on the great hinge of the incarnation of the Son of God, and the redeeming work of Christ rests on the fact that on the third day he rose from the dead.

The Testimony of Scripture

The Gospels unapologetically affirm and narrate the bodily resurrection of Jesus. Each of the Gospel writers—Matthew, Mark, Luke, and John—wrote about the empty tomb, the witnesses, and the appearances of the risen Christ. The book of Acts portrays the cross and resurrection as central to the apostolic preaching in the early church. Furthermore, the epistles expand upon the theological implications of the resurrection. The entire substance of New Testament theology finds its ultimate expression in the resurrection of Jesus Christ.

Each of the four biblical Gospels presents a consistent witness to the bodily resurrection of Jesus. While the first to bear witness of the empty tomb may have conveyed confusion about this unexpected event, the fourfold Gospel lens records with clarity the historicity of the resurrection in Matthew 28, Mark 16, Luke 24, and John 20. After the first two witnesses—two women—returned from the empty tomb, their words about the resurrection seemed like nonsense to the disciples. Peter then investigated the empty tomb himself. After examining the empty tomb, he departed, wondering what had happened (Luke

24:12). Jesus himself enters the narrative later in Luke when he encounters two men and says:

> "O foolish ones, and slow of heart to believe all that the prophets have spoken! Was it not necessary that the Christ should suffer these things and enter into his glory?" And beginning with Moses and all the Prophets, he interpreted to them in all the Scriptures the things concerning himself. (Luke 24:25–27)

While this rebuke from Jesus seems forceful, the words vindicate his resurrection and demonstrate it was a fulfillment of prophetic expectation. His disciples should have expected his resurrection because Jesus spoke of it often (Matt. 17:22; 26:61; Mark 8:31; 14:58; Luke 9:22; John 2:19). The Gospels consistently witness to the historical, bodily resurrection of Jesus from the dead.

Furthermore, Christ and his resurrection energized and validated the message of the apostles and the early church. Early in the book of Acts, Peter boldly proclaimed his assurance that Christ was the divine Savior precisely because God raised him from the dead: "God raised him up, loosing the pangs of death, because it was not possible for him to be held by it" (Acts 2:24). For Peter and the other disciples, the resurrection of Jesus vindicated his position as the promised heir who would sit on the Davidic throne (Acts 2:29–36). Peter's sermon at the beginning of Acts models the twofold apostolic proclamation: the cross and the resurrection. In fact, sinners are called to faith and repentance precisely because of the cross and the resurrection. Peter preached to the Gentiles and made this connection between the cross, resurrection, and repentance:

They put him to death by hanging him on a tree, but God
raised him on the third day and made him to appear . . . .
And he commanded us to preach to the people and to testify that [Jesus] is the one appointed by God to be judge of
the living and the dead. To him all the prophets bear witness
that everyone who believes in him receives forgiveness of sins
through his name. (Acts 10:39–43)

Peter understood that the resurrection secures the hope
of salvation. Also, near the end of Acts, Paul confirmed this
understanding by formulating a clear correlation between the
resurrection of Jesus and the forgiveness of sins: "But he whom
God raised up did not see corruption. Let it be known to you
therefore, brothers, that through this man forgiveness of sins
is proclaimed to you" (Acts 13:37–38). The resurrection of
Christ was not just an essential doctrine to the early church;
rather, Christ's resurrection lies at the heart of the apostolic
proclamation—and the witness of the church today.

Paul and the other New Testament writers taught on the
resurrection at length. Paul did not mince words when he considered the theological necessity of the resurrection: "If Christ
has not been raised, your faith is futile and you are still in your
sins" (1 Cor. 15:17). However, the death and resurrection of
Christ together saves all those who were subject to death and
decay (cf. Heb. 2:14–15). In other words, because of the resurrection of Christ, all those who were dead in sins have hope of a
new life: "For as by a man came death, by a man has come also
the resurrection of the dead. For as in Adam all die, so also in
Christ shall all be made alive" (1 Cor. 15:21–22). As a result,
Paul observed that God raised Jesus "for our justification" (Rom.
4:25; cf. Rom. 10:9–10). Jesus died to pay for human sin and was

raised to accomplish justification; indeed, because Jesus did not remain dead, Christians do not remain in their sins.

Peter also highlighted the resurrection of Christ in the context of our salvation: "Blessed be the God and Father of our Lord Jesus Christ! According to his great mercy, he has caused us to be born again to a living hope through the resurrection of Jesus Christ from the dead" (1 Peter 1:3). Christians, in their regeneration, experience the same resurrection power that brought Christ from the dead. We can be born again because Jesus Christ is risen from the grave.

After examining a fraction of the New Testament passages that mention the resurrection, consider a few of the major themes that have been noted by these passages.

- First, the cross and the resurrection represent a unified saving action (Rom. 4:24–25).
- Second, as a promise of the future, the church preaches the *bodily* resurrection of Christ from the dead (Luke 24:24).
- Third, the bodily resurrection of Christ fulfills the promises of God in the Old Testament (Luke 24:25–27).
- Fourth, the resurrection of Christ from the dead provides the ground of our salvation since he lives always to make intercession (Heb. 7:25).
- Fifth, the resurrection of Christ is an incentive to repentance (Acts 10:39–43; 13:37–38).
- Sixth, Christians experience the same resurrection power in sanctification (1 Peter 1:3).
- Seventh, the resurrection identifies Jesus Christ as the true Son of God (Acts 17:30–31). The resurrection of Christ is not merely one doctrine among others—it is of the highest doctrinal importance.

Remember how the apostle Paul began that great chapter on the resurrection:

> Now I would remind you, brothers, of the gospel I preached to you, which you received, in which you stand, and by which you are being saved, if you hold fast to the word I preached to you—unless you believed in vain. (1 Cor. 15:1–2)

This is the gospel that saves, Paul stated boldly, unless you believed in vain. What would this mean, believing in vain? Paul went on to explain that if Christ has not been raised bodily from the grave, we are still dead in our sins. "And if Christ has not been raised, your faith is futile and you are still in your sins" (1 Cor. 15:17).

He continued to make the issue clear: "If in Christ we have hope in this life only, we are of all people most to be pitied" (1 Cor. 15:19). So this is why Paul, putting the cross and resurrection at the very center of the gospel, emphasized the theological priorities:

> For I delivered to you as of first importance what I also received: that Christ died for our sins in accordance with the Scriptures, that he was buried, that he was raised on the third day in accordance with the Scriptures. (1 Cor. 15:3–4)

Look clearly at the language Paul used here—of *first importance* and *according to the Scriptures*. The apostle gets our attention and makes us face the reality of the gospel and the centrality of both the cross and the empty tomb. Here we see as well that the words of the Apostles' Creed are drawn directly from the Bible.

Theological Significance

To further illustrate the theological centrality of the resurrection, consider three dimensions of the theological significance of the resurrection. First, through the resurrection, Christians find *justification*. The Father justifies or vindicates the Son by accepting the sacrifice of the Son on behalf of Christians, and the Father demonstrates this vindication through the resurrection. Therefore, the resurrection provides proof that the atonement Jesus made was accepted by the Father (Rom. 4:24–25; Phil. 2:8–9).

Second, the Bible depicts regeneration as the result of resurrection power. Paul prayed that the Ephesians would know "the immeasurable greatness of his power toward us" and wrote that this power was revealed "when he raised him from the dead" (Eph. 1:19–20). Also, in their union with Christ, the resurrection power transforms the life of the Christian into greater conformity with Christ (Rom. 6:3–5, 8; 1 Cor. 15:20–23; Eph. 1:18–20). Calvin helpfully characterized the resurrection in terms of both justification and regeneration:

Sin was taken away by his death; righteousness was revived and restored by his resurrection. For how could he by dying have freed us from death if he had himself succumbed to death? How could he have acquired victory for us if he had failed in the struggle? Therefore, we divide the substance of our salvation between Christ's death and resurrection as follows: through his death, sin was wiped out and death extinguished; through his resurrection, righteousness was restored and life raised up, so that—thanks to his resurrection—his death manifested its power and efficacy in us.[1]

Indeed the New Testament, the source of Calvin's theology, routinely applies resurrection terminology to the regeneration of the Christian. Peter, like Paul, associated regeneration language with Christ's resurrection. Christians were made "to be born again to a living hope through the resurrection of Jesus Christ from the dead." Christ's resurrection provides the source of new spiritual life—new life is a sharing of Christ's resurrection life (1 Peter 1:3).

Third, the resurrection of Christ portends a great eschatological glorification of God's people. In fact, the resurrection of Jesus itself represents an eschatological event and signifies the beginning of the eschatological resurrection for all Christians:

> Glorification is the final step in the application of redemption. It will happen when Christ returns and raises from the dead the bodies of believers for all time who have died, and reunites them with their souls, and changes the bodies of believers who remain alive, thereby giving all believers at the same time perfect resurrection bodies like his own.[2]

Paul indicated that the resurrection of Christ symbolizes the "firstborn from the dead" (Col. 1:18). As a result, Christ's resurrection foreshadows the corporate resurrection of his people. Also, Christ's resurrection is the "firstfruits" of those who have fallen asleep (1 Cor. 15:20, 23), and the term "firstfruits" (Rom. 8:23; 11:16; 16:5) guarantees that more will come. Furthermore, Jesus Christ, as the "last Adam" and "a life-giving spirit" (1 Cor. 15:45), signifies that Christ is the creator of a new race of people—a people outside of the headship of Adam. Adam passed on to mankind "the image of the man of dust," but in Jesus, Christians will one day bear the likeness of the "man of heaven" (1 Cor. 15:49).

The bodily resurrection of Jesus Christ from the dead provides the assurance that those who believe in him will also be raised from the dead. Paul wrote:

I tell you this, brothers: flesh and blood cannot inherit the kingdom of God, nor does the perishable inherit the imperishable. Behold! I tell you a mystery. We shall not all sleep, but we shall all be changed, in a moment, in the twinkling of an eye, at the last trumpet. For the trumpet will sound, and the dead will be raised imperishable, and we shall be changed. For this perishable body must put on the imperishable, and this mortal body must put on immortality. When the perishable puts on the imperishable, and the mortal puts on immortality, then shall come to pass the saying that is written:

"Death is swallowed up in victory."
"O death, where is your victory?
O death, where is your sting?"
The sting of death is sin, and the power of sin is the law.
(1 Cor. 15:50–56)

This is why Christians love to sing about the risen Christ. If Christ's body stayed in the tomb, sin would still have us in its fell grip.

Conclusion

Christ's resurrection establishes the theological foundation upon which the Christian finds forgiveness of sins, deliverance from death, and life everlasting. We can now see why the empty tomb is the source of such hope and the assurance of our salvation. The resurrection of Christ from the dead fulfilled all the promises of God. Now Christians can look forward to the end of time when Christ will destroy death forever—an action he began with his resurrection from the dead. The Father has announced to all creation, in heaven and on earth, that Jesus Christ is the risen Lord.

CHAPTER NINE

HE ASCENDED INTO HEAVEN AND SITS AT THE RIGHT HAND OF GOD

I f the Apostles' Creed omitted Jesus' ascension into heaven and his place at the right hand of the Father, would you have noticed? A wealth of Christian literature and devotion centers on the cross of Christ and all that Jesus accomplished in his sacrifice as well as on his resurrection from the dead. The emphasis on the second coming also marks a foundation of Christian spirituality and hope. Christ's ascension into heaven, however, finds little or no recognition among many contemporary Christians. Few sermons from pulpits explain the incalculable riches of Christ's ascension into heaven. We sing few, if any, hymns on the ascension of Christ. Christians fail to meditate on and apply in their lives the glorious reality of Jesus enthroned on high with the cosmos at his feet.

Without the ascension of Jesus, the gospel possesses no present power. When Jesus sat down at the right hand of God, he inaugurated a new age of hope founded upon his completed ministry. Indeed, this thunderous component of the Apostles' Creed affirms essential truths, without which the church could not possibly stand. Christians must, therefore, orient their lives around the splendor of Christ's ascension into heaven and his coronation as King of the universe. These two truths should stand as a beacon of Christian spirituality. Few words should be as comforting to the Christian as "He ascended into heaven and sits at the right hand of God."

What Does the Bible Say About the Ascension?

The framers of the creed penned into its affirmations only what they understood as essential to the Christian faith. The Bible, therefore, served as the source of their work in delineating the fundamentals of Christian theology, doctrine, and worship. The assertion that Jesus ascended into heaven and sits enthroned at God's right hand made its way into the creed because of its significance to the New Testament and to the faith of the church.

The gospels of Mark and Luke contain the fullest and most detailed accounts of Jesus' ascension. Luke also included the ascension in the book of Acts. While Matthew and John provided no explicit account of the ascension, it nonetheless permeates as a theme of their gospel narratives. Matthew's gospel centers on the inauguration of the new kingdom under Jesus Christ and points to his ascension to God's right hand. Indeed, the Great Commission in Matthew 28 contains sweet promises of Jesus to his disciples. He promised his enduring presence with them throughout the end of the ages and that all authority in heaven and on earth belongs to him. John 3:13 and the entirety of John 14 speak of Jesus' coming ascension and heavenly reign then yet to come.

The gospels of Mark, Luke, and the book of Acts, however, contain explicit historical accounts of the final moments of Jesus' time on earth with his disciples:

- "While he blessed them, he parted from them and was carried up into heaven. And they worshiped him and returned to Jerusalem with great joy, and were continually in the temple blessing God." (Luke 24:51–53)
- "So then the Lord Jesus, after he had spoken to them, was taken up into heaven and sat down at the right hand of God. And they went out and preached everywhere, while the Lord worked with them and confirmed the message by accompanying signs." (Mark 16:19–20)
- "'But you will receive power when the Holy Spirit has come upon you . . .' And when he had said these things, as they were looking on, he was lifted up, and a cloud took him out of their sight." (Acts 1:8–9)

These three accounts testify to the intimacy and drama of Christ's final moments with his disciples. Mark and Luke recorded this event for the benefit of the whole church. Their narratives preserve the beauty this moment encapsulates and the hope that Christians have in the eternal reign of Christ over the creation. Christ's ascension reveals three pillars that are essential to Christian theology. First, the ascension of Christ grounds his exaltation. Second, the ascension establishes the giving of the Holy Spirit. Finally, the ascension secured a place for Christians in heaven for all eternity.

Christ's Exaltation

I had a dear friend who served as a trustee for the Southern Baptist Theological Seminary. Mr. Glenn Miles lived in Crystal Springs, Mississippi. He used to keep asking me, "When are you going to come up to see us?" I thought he was wrong. Simple geography would suggest that my position in Louisville, Kentucky, would mean I would travel not up, but down. I said, "Mr. Miles, I'll have to come *down* and see you." He said, "No, young man. Everything's down from Crystal Springs, Mississippi." We get the point. Mr. Miles understood his tiny patch of land in Mississippi as sacred, honored, and above all else on earth.

God ordained the ascension to exalt Jesus above all creation. In each of the ascension narratives, Christ goes *up* to heaven. Luke's account uses the language of being "carried up into heaven" (24:51). This ascent, more than a spatial progression from earth to heaven, enshrines the glory, supremacy, and exaltation of Jesus Christ. The Father received his Son back to his throne of glory. Paul revealed the exaltation of Christ after his ascension:

> He raised [Christ] from the dead and seated him at his right hand in the heavenly places, far above all rule and authority and power and dominion, and above every name that is named, not only in this age but also in the one to come. And he put all things under his feet and gave him as head over all

things to the church, which is his body, the fullness of him who fills all in all. (Eph. 1:20–23)

The Father raised Jesus from the dead to seat him at his right hand. This seat represents the place of supreme authority over the entire creation. The largest star and the unseen atom come under the rule of Jesus Christ. Every throne on earth, every king in authority, every power in the cosmos, submits to the reign of the One who conquered the grave.

The seating of Christ at the right hand of God underlines Christ's present reign and his continuing work on behalf of believers. The risen and exalted Christ is Prophet, Priest, and King. As our Great High Priest, he intercedes for believers before the Father. He is eternally and perfectly our Mediator before the Father. As we read in Hebrews 7:25, "Consequently, he is able to save to the uttermost those who draw near to God through him, since he always lives to make intercession for them." As much as we needed Christ's substitutionary atonement on the cross, we also need his intercession before the Father. Our salvation depends upon his faithfulness as our Mediator and Great High Priest—sitting at the right hand of the Father.

Paul also wrote of Christ's exaltation in his rich christological hymn found in Philippians 2:9–11. In that passage Paul wrote that God has "highly exalted" Jesus. His exaltation contains such power that even the proclamation of his name prostrates all creation before his glory and his throne. One day, every tongue, every tribe, every nation, will resound in unity to declare the lordship of Jesus Christ. The ascension of Christ, therefore, serves as a cosmic coronation whereby God the Father confirms Christ's sacrifice and subjects the universe to his rule.

Without the ascension Jesus would not be ruling *right now*

at the right hand of God the Father. After Jesus completed his work and obeyed the will of his Father, even unto death, the heavenly courts welcomed him home in celestial beauty. The Father exalted his Son and seated him on the throne that is above every throne. Jesus declared, "It is finished" (John 19:30), and the Father then raised him from the dead and received him back. This truth establishes the hope of every follower of Jesus Christ. Without his ascension, exaltation, and coronation, Jesus would possess no authority to rule, and ultimately, to reconcile all things to himself (Col. 1:18–20). In short there would be no gospel to proclaim.

The Giving of the Holy Spirit

When Jesus ascended to heaven, he did not leave his disciples alone in the world. Indeed, the ascension secured a peculiar power that Christians in every age would know and depend upon. Without this power Christians would fail in their faith, remain defenseless against Satan, and have no assurance in their status as children of God. Through Jesus' ascension he gave the church the Holy Spirit.

When Jesus told his disciples of his impending departure, he comforted them with this astounding assertion: "Nevertheless, I tell you the truth: *it is to your advantage that I go away*, for if I do not go away, the Helper will not come to you" (John 16:7). Jesus communicated the disadvantage to his disciples and the church if he *did not* ascend into heaven. Without his ascension the Spirit could not come; and, in some mysterious, spectacular way, the indwelling of the Spirit eclipses the physical presence of Jesus Christ.

Jesus tells his disciples their need for the coming of the Spirit and their need for Jesus to ascend. Jesus gave three reasons why his ascension and the subsequent giving of the Spirit marks a glorious turning point for his disciples and the church (John 16:13–14).

1. "When the Spirit of truth comes, he will guide you into all the truth." When Jesus ascends, the Spirit will come and bear witness to the truth. Jesus knew his disciples would face tumultuous times, fierce persecutions, and seemingly insurmountable theological obstacles. The Spirit, however, will guide the church in the truth of Christ and preserve them from the danger of doctrinal error.

2. "He will declare to you the things that are to come." Not only will the Spirit guide the disciples in the truth, he will reveal the eschatological hope for the church. This revelation, enshrined in the Scriptures, will guide the church throughout every age. The future glories of the final victory of Christ shine as a brilliant light for every believer.

3. "He will take what is mine and declare it to you." The Holy Spirit proclaims the word of Christ to the people of Christ. The Spirit, therefore, brings the direct revelation of God to the church. He does this for their health and survival as pilgrims, passing by on their way to the celestial city. Without the Spirit's revelation of the things of Christ, the church would have no word to guide them, no instruction by which to live, no truth upon which to build their hope. The church received from the Spirit the inspired Word of God that guides believers in every facet of their discipleship. The ascension of Christ, therefore, assured the fullness of God's revelation to his church, which he communicated through the power and ministry of the Spirit. This communication came to the church in the form of the Bible—the Spirit-inspired Word of God.

Seen in this light, the ascension of Christ provided for the church the gift of the Holy Spirit. Jesus revealed to his disciples that without his ascension, the Holy Spirit would not come and fulfill his crucial and necessary role for the people of God. Christians today must recognize the significant connection between Christ's ascension and the ministry of the Holy Spirit. Without the former the latter could not become a reality. Without the latter the church could not have survived—nor could the church survive even now.

The Eternal Dwelling of God's People

Finally, the ascension of Christ secures the eternal dwelling place of God's people in heaven. Jesus comforted his disciples on his coming departure with words of incalculable assurance (John 14:1–4). He told the disciples that when he departs, he goes to prepare a place for the people of God. Indeed, Jesus said, "In my Father's house are many rooms. If it were not so, would I have told you that I go to prepare a place for you?" (John 14:2). Jesus, therefore, informed his church that he must depart not only for his exaltation but also for the giving of the Spirit. Jesus' ascension paved the way for the eternal resting place of the household of faith.

Jesus did not ascend to heaven to become idle. He actively prepares a home for all his followers on earth. Jesus secured the down payment with his blood. All who repent of their sins and place their faith in Christ partake in this rich blessing and become citizens of the heavenly kingdom. Christians often fail to recognize the unfathomable glories of grace that Christ revealed (John 14). He grounded our future hope in heaven with his ascension to the right hand of the Father. His present reign serves as a reminder for all believers that their citizenship rests in heaven.

Jesus focused not on the "rooms" in the Father's house; rather, he communicated the blessed and eternal communion and fellowship that will exist between Christ and his people. Jesus said, "I will come again and will take you to myself, that where I am you may be also" (John 14:3). Thus, Jesus' ascension secured an intimate fellowship with God himself in the age to come. This truth provides incomparable comfort to all those who believe in Jesus Christ. Paul said, "For you have died, and your life is hidden with Christ in God" (Col. 3:3). The intimacy of this language should astound all who know their sin and yet have discovered the immeasurable grace of God. Christians everywhere glory in the inheritance that Jesus Christ himself prepares for them—for us, together, as Christ's people.

A Theology of Ascension

Thus far, we explored what the Bible reveals about Christ's ascension and the glories of his heavenly reign. The reason so few Christians contemplate Christ's ascension stems from a deficient theology of ascension and the myriad crucial doctrines connected to this affirmation in the Apostles' Creed. Indeed, the doctrine of Christ's ascension functions as a vital foundation upon which the entire Christian gospel stands. Without its support we have no assurance in the present and no hope for the future. Specifically, the doctrines of Christ's vindication, the reality of heaven, and our union with Christ, flow powerfully from the confession, "He ascended into heaven and sits at the right hand of God."

The Vindication of Jesus

The ascension of Jesus manifests the seal of God's approval for all that Christ has done. The Father receives the Son back with joy because Jesus accomplished perfectly all the commands of his Father. The dying words of Jesus, "It is finished," contain both excruciating grief and surpassing victory. Grief because the Son of God hung on the cross, murdered by wicked men. The sins of God's people held him there. At the same time "It is finished" amounts to a resounding declaration of victory—a victory over death, the Devil, and the realization of all God's promises accomplished through Christ. After Jesus' ascension the Father seated his Son at his right hand and showed his affirmation of the life and ministry of Christ. Specifically, God the Father sent Jesus to accomplish the establishment of the new kingdom and the salvation of sinners.

In his first sermon on earth, Jesus proclaimed, "The time is fulfilled, and the kingdom of God is at hand; repent and believe in the gospel" (Mark 1:15). Through his incarnation, Jesus brought God's kingdom to fulfillment. Christ's ascension marks a glorious moment for this new kingdom. While on earth, the incarnate Christ began to reverse the effects of the curse. The blind could see, the lame could walk, and the dead rose from the grave. He also espoused the right teaching and full revelation of God's promises in the Old Testament. He taught their true meaning and lifted from the scriptural instruction the weights and traditions placed there by the scribes and Pharisees. When Jesus came, he came to establish a new kingdom—a reign that would make all things new; a reign that would span eternity.

Christ's ascension bears the fruit of this new kingdom. The first fruits have come, yet its fullness has yet to be realized. The phrase *inaugurated eschatology* defines the age in which we live. The church lives in the "already-but-not-yet" reality of the kingdom. The ministry of Jesus and his ascension to the throne of heaven inaugurated the new eternal reign of Christ's kingdom and established the new covenant. This new kingdom, however, has not yet fully come into realization.

Despite the "already-but-not-yet" age in which we live, Jesus' ascension marks the vindication of his time here on earth as God seated him on the celestial throne. This vindication inaugurated a new age in the earth, an age where the new creation has broken in, the curses of the fall have been reversed, and Christ sits over the cosmos having crushed the head of the serpent. His vindication through the kingdom will come fully when this earth passes away and the words of Revelation 21:3–4 become reality: We will dwell with God and he will dwell with us. God will wipe away every tear. Death will be dead. Mourning shall cease. Pain will be forgotten. The old will be made new.

Also, through the obedient life, death, and resurrection of Jesus, salvation has come to sinners. Jesus summarized his purpose of coming to earth: "For the Son of Man came to seek and to save the lost" (Luke 19:10). From eternity past God purposed to redeem sinners by the blood of Jesus Christ (Eph. 1:3–9). Though the cross brought agony and suffering to Jesus, it brought eternal comfort and joy to Christians and secured our salvation from sin.

Had Christ not ascended into heaven, however, Christians would still be dead in their sins. The ascension of Christ thundered from the heavens as God's approval of the ministry of Christ. The church can rest in comfort in the forgiveness of sins because God raised Christ from the dead and seated him on the throne of heaven. The Father vindicated the Son and this vindication serves as a seal upon the forgiveness of sins. God sent Jesus to redeem his people. Jesus' ascension marks the sure foundation and accomplishment of that work.

Jesus Christ came to earth to establish a kingdom and to redeem a people. What do these two things have to do with his ascension? The ascension proclaims the certainty of the kingdom and the sufficiency of the sacrificial work of Christ. The ascension communicates the Father's approval of these accomplishments of Christ. Thus, the kingdom that Christ inaugurated will never cease to exist. What God established and decreed will never fail (Num. 23:19). Also, by receiving his Son, the Father accepted the sacrifice of Jesus as a payment for sin. The Father declared the cross as sufficient. This means that when a sinner "repents and believes the gospel," he will be called a child of God. The ascension revealed God's vindication of the earthly work of Christ. Without the ascension Christians could not live in confidence of the eternality of the kingdom and the sufficiency of the cross.

The Reality of Heaven

In Mark's account of the ascension, he wrote, "So then the Lord Jesus, after he had spoken to them, was taken up into heaven and sat down at the right hand of God" (16:19). Mark clearly identified a specific location to which Jesus ascended. Jesus' ascension, therefore, provided further grounding for a literal location of heaven—the dwelling place of God, the heavenly host, and his people.

Some people and groups view heaven or the afterlife as a state of mind or an attitude. These individuals reject heaven as a physical or literal place. The Scriptures, however, speak of heaven not with *subjective language* but as an *objective location*. Heaven exists as a reality and place to which all who believe in Christ will one day live for all eternity. The Bible does not disclose heaven's location. Many passages, however, describe it with directional language: Christ ascended to it (Mark 16:19), the Holy Spirit descended from it (Matt. 3:16), and Enoch was taken up into heaven by a chariot (2 Kings 2:11).

Heaven marks the resting place of God's people, where, for all eternity, we will commune with God face-to-face. The radiance of God's glory fills the heavenly places and believers in Christ will bask in all its beauty. This ought to encourage Christians who live in the "already-but-not-yet" kingdom on earth. Though Christians endure suffering, persecution, and the effects of sin, we do so with sure hope. We rest in the promises of the Bible that describe believers as "called . . . to his eternal glory in Christ" who will "restore, confirm, strengthen, and establish" them (1 Peter 5:10). This objective place called heaven contains the inheritance by which all Christians will fully experience the glory of the Lord forever.

Our Union with Christ

Finally, Jesus' ascension deepens our understanding of our union with him. From the moment of faith, Christians receive the benefits of salvation for all eternity. Theologian Wayne Grudem wrote, "We are in Christ, Christ is in us, we are like Christ, and we are with Christ."[1] Thus, in the eyes of God, we have been buried and raised with Christ (Rom. 6:5). Jesus' death becomes ours. His resurrection becomes our resurrection. His inheritance becomes our inheritance.

As Christ ascended into heaven, he demonstrated the infinite glories of our union with him. Particularly, Jesus revealed the integral connection between his ascension and our reign with him for all eternity. Paul described the reign of Christians by virtue of our union to Jesus. He wrote,

> But God, being rich in mercy, because of the great love with which he loved us, even when we were dead in our trespasses, made us alive together with Christ—by grace you have been

saved—and raised us up with him and seated us with him in the heavenly places in Christ Jesus. (Eph. 2:4–6)

As God put all things under Jesus' authority, we, too, become coheirs with Christ by our union with him (Rom. 8:17). Christians reign with Christ and will reign fully after his second coming. In the current age Christians rule with Christ despite not being physically with the Lord in heaven. God has received his Son and welcomed him to a seat of authority, and thus, by virtue of our union, Grudem explains that we, too, "share in some measure in the authority that Christ has, authority to contend against the spiritual hosts of wickedness in the heavenly places (Eph. 6:12) and to do battle with weapons that have divine power to destroy strongholds (2 Cor. 10:4)."[2]

At the second coming of Jesus, however, the fullness of our reign with Christ will shine in resplendent beauty. Christians will be the ones who "have authority over the nations" (Rev. 2:26–27) and judge the angels (1 Cor. 6:3). Jesus himself said to the church in Laodicea, "The one who conquers, I will grant him to sit with me on my throne, as I also conquered and sat down with my Father on his throne" (Rev. 3:21). Thus, just as Christ ascended and sits on the heavenly throne, the Father will usher his people to a glorious seat of authority because of their union with Christ.

Applying the Truth

The biblical and theological currents of Christ's ascension and celestial reign should draw all Christians to a state of gratitude and worship. The ascension of Jesus bears incalculable implications for the gospel and its promises.

The Certainty of Salvation

The ascension of Christ provides an immovable foundation and security in our salvation. Jesus' ascension marks the seal of the Father's pleasure on his ministry. When the Father carried Jesus into heaven, he declared forever the efficacy of Christ's sacrifice. When the Father seated Jesus at his right hand, all things came under Jesus' subjection and rule. Nothing in all creation lives outside of his reign. The ascension of Jesus, therefore, establishes assurance of salvation and the surety of the perseverance of the saints. Christians can rest in the knowledge of Christ's ascension because we know of the Savior's completed and continuing work and his eternal rule over the cosmos.

The Means to Live Boldly

Finally, because Christ ascended to heaven, Christians can live boldly for the glory of God. The Scriptures encourage us, saying that we can "with confidence draw near to the throne of grace, that we may receive mercy and find grace to help in time of need" (Heb. 4:16). Our unity with Christ, our Mediator and Great High Priest, provides direct access to God the Father. The surety of our unity flows from Christ's ascension and enthronement. There, in the heavenly courts, Jesus intercedes for his people (Rom. 8:34). His ascension and rule, therefore, energizes a Christian spirituality of boldness. The One who paid the debt of our sin sits enthroned over all the creation. Death could not hold him in the grave. He rose from the dead, ascended into heaven, and sits as King of kings and Lord of lords. Christians can live boldly because our God has in Christ accomplished the work, finished the task, and rules over all by his providential care.

Conclusion

When Jesus ascended to heaven, he left his followers with a promise and an assignment. He promised the gift of the Holy Spirit to help them to understand truth and to live lives of obedience. Jesus assigned them to "go and make disciples of all nations" (Matt. 28:19 NIV). The ascension of Jesus makes this task possible. Without his ascension the Spirit would not have come. Without his reign at the right hand of God, the Christian would face insurmountable obstacles and overwhelming satanic opposition. Christ, however, did ascend. Christ, however, does reign in absolute authority.

The ascension of Jesus marked his exaltation and vindication. The entirety of his ministry culminated in his ascension, a watershed event that became the seal of the Father's pleasure on all Christ accomplished. Thus, Jesus' ascension secured the eternal dwelling place of God's people and points to the reality of heaven as the place where God and his people will rest together forever.

The reality of Christ's ascension and celestial enthronement enshrines all the hopes, expectations, and promises of the gospel. Indeed, without the truths associated with this affirmation, there would in fact be no good news to proclaim in the gospel. Yet, good news has come, for Christ ascended into heaven, marking his ultimate defeat over death. Good news has come, for Christ sits enthroned and inaugurated a new kingdom, a new age, a new day of salvation for the people of God. And the One who is ascended to the Father and now sits at his right hand is the very Christ who commissioned his church to go into all the nations and make disciples, "baptizing them in the name of the Father and of the Son and of the Holy Spirit, teaching them to observe all that I have commanded you." That same Christ then gave the church this promise: "And behold, I am with you always, to the end of the age" (Matt. 28:19–20).

CHAPTER TEN

WHENCE HE SHALL COME TO JUDGE THE QUICK AND THE DEAD

To be human is to be a narrative creature. From the earliest days of our lives, we understand that every story worth telling or worth hearing has a beginning, middle, and end. So many of the stories we are told at a young age begin with "Once upon a time" and end with "They all lived happily ever after." We crave resolution to our stories.

The temporal aspect of humanity requires us to understand that there is an end to which history is headed, an end to our story as we know it. As temporal creatures, we are limited by a span of life and thus, even as we live in a frame of the past, present, and future, there is an end to which our lives are heading. Regardless of our worldview, eschatology—belief about the future—plays a vital role in every human life. Everyone has some vision of the future, and we live our lives in light of it.

Rival Eschatologies

Every worldview, not just Christianity, makes an argument about how history will end. Every worldview has to have *some* explanation for what will happen to the cosmos and a view about that end's significance. Throughout Western civilization Christianity has had a greater influence on eschatological views than has any other worldview—and Christianity's eschatology reveals a final judgment.

A rival to Christian eschatology arose with the secularization of Western culture over the last two centuries. Secularists deny any supernatural elements to the universe. Therefore, they assume that the energy in the cosmos will dissipate into nonenergy, and, as a result, everything will eventually fade into oblivion. The great question for most secularists is not whether there will be an end, but whether it will be a bang or a whimper. Will it be the slow, inexorable slide from being into nonbeing and energy into entropy? Or will it be something cataclysmic—a conclusion that mirrors the beginning of our universe with the "big bang"? Is the end just eternal silence as all matter collapses within a black hole?

Yearnings for the Future

No matter our worldview, human beings have an instinctive yearning to know the future and to live our lives in light of the future. We understand the present through recollection of the past and anticipatory hope for the future. This understanding of the future is necessary in order to understand how we can live, how we can love, how we can hope, and how we can be faithful in the present. Both past and future explain the present.

Scripture provides us with a grand metanarrative that takes us from creation to new creation. The Christian gospel is expressed as a story—past, present, and future. The past: our sin and what God has done for us in and through Christ. The present: how we are to respond to what God has accomplished for us in Christ. And the future: how we are to hope with confidence as we anticipate the fulfillment of all God's promises. The Apostles' Creed reflects this same future orientation in the words: *whence he shall come to judge the quick and the dead.*

Up to this point most of the creed has been in the past tense. "He *was conceived* by the Holy Ghost, [*was*] *born* of the Virgin Mary, *suffered* under Pontius Pilate, *was crucified*, dead, and buried. He *descended* into hell. The third day he *rose* again from the dead. He *ascended* into heaven." All of that is history. As we look at the Christian story, all those facets of the gospel are in the past. That is God's provision for us in space, time, and history through Christ.

Then the creed moves to the present tense, which is reflected in the work of Christ for us now. He reigns as Prophet, Priest, and King—as our mediator before the Father. He "sits at the right hand of God the Father Almighty." And then the creed moves to the future tense: "whence he *shall come* to judge the quick and the dead."

The story of the Bible is framed by its eschatology, expressing God's glory in his dealings with humanity with respect to a complete timeline. We move from creation to fall to redemption to consummation; and if any one of these chapters in God's great work were missing or minimized, we lose the comprehensive glory of God that is found in the gospel of Jesus Christ.

On the other side of Genesis 3, there is implanted within our hearts and souls a yearning that orients our gaze upon the provision God has made for us in the future. As Israel longed for the Messiah, so all humanity was and is desiring even now salvation from the pains of this world—a desire that can only truly be realized through faith in Christ and the eventual establishment of his kingdom in glory. We yearn for the consummation of our salvation (John 10:28). We are told that Christ came not only to "bear the sins of many," but he will also "appear a second time, not to deal with sin but to save those who are eagerly waiting for him" (Heb. 9:28). In this promise every human yearning will be fulfilled.

Thus, Christians do not merely put their hope in Christ and then go about living according to the passions of their former ignorance. Every believer is urged to "set your hope fully on the grace that will be brought to you at the revelation of Jesus Christ" (1 Peter 1:13). The gravity of this hope necessitates that life be lived with great anticipation—and confidence in Christ.

Judgment

Jesus taught us to set our minds on the blessed hope and the coming judgment:

> "From the fig tree learn its lesson: as soon as its branch becomes tender and puts out its leaves, you know that summer is near. So also, when you see all these things, you know that he is near, at the very gates. Truly, I say to you, this generation will not pass away until all these things take place. Heaven and earth will pass away, but my words will not pass away.

"But concerning that day and hour no one knows, not even the angels of heaven, nor the Son, but the Father only. For as were the days of Noah, so will be the coming of the Son of Man. For as in those days before the flood they were eating and drinking, marrying and giving in marriage, until the day when Noah entered the ark, and they were unaware until the flood came and swept them all away, so will be the coming of the Son of Man. Then two men will be in the field; one will be taken and one left. Two women will be grinding at the mill; one will be taken and one left. Therefore, stay awake, for you do not know on what day your Lord is coming." (Matt. 24:32–42)

He continued:

"When the Son of Man comes in his glory, and all the angels with him, then he will sit on his glorious throne. Before him will be gathered all the nations, and he will separate people one from another as a shepherd separates the sheep from the goats. And he will place the sheep on his right, but the goats on the left. Then the King will say to those on his right, 'Come, you who are blessed by my Father, inherit the kingdom prepared for you from the foundation of the world.'" (Matt. 25:31–34)

Later in the same chapter, Jesus warns about the judgment, "Then he will say to those on his left, 'Depart from me, you cursed, into the eternal fire prepared for the devil and his angels'" (Matt. 25:41).

These passages clearly affirm that Christ will return in judgment upon sinners, which is why the creed states, "whence he

shall come *to judge* the quick and the dead." Christ is coming—
and he is coming to judge.

In his first coming Christ came as Savior and Redeemer. He
came "conceived of the Holy Spirit, born of the Virgin Mary."
He came as a lowly infant. History at that moment hardly noticed
this child Messiah wrapped in swaddling cloth, lying in a manger.
The announcement of his arrival was made only to lowly shepherds nearby. When he came the first time, he came in humility.
But when he comes from where he is now seated at the right hand
of God, things will be very different. When he comes as the crucified, resurrected, and ascended Lord, he will come as the One
to whom every knee shall bow! He will come as the One whom
every tongue will confess as Lord.

Part of God's vindication of his Son is that the One who was
so wrongly judged by humanity will now come to execute righteous judgment upon every single human being. The One who
was judged will be the Judge. Scripture speaks of the judgment
seat of God. It speaks of that day as the "great and terrible day
of the LORD" (Joel 2:31 CSB). But Scripture also makes clear that
Jesus is the agent of that judgment. In John's gospel we read,
"the Father judges no one, but has given all judgment to the Son"
(John 5:22). Paul told the Athenians, "He has fixed a day on
which he will judge the world in righteousness by a man whom
he has appointed; and of this he has given assurance to all by
raising him from the dead" (Acts 17:31). Paul also referred to the
Lord Jesus Christ as the "righteous judge" (2 Tim. 4:8) and spoke
of the "judgment seat of Christ" (2 Cor. 5:10) before which we
all must appear. The language of the Bible is clear and consistent.
Christ will come to judge all humanity, and no one escapes his
judgment—*no one*.

The Father's good pleasure with the Son is not only that the fullness of the Godhead dwelt within him; but it is the Father's plan and desire that the fullness of the Godhead be displayed in the end of all history when the Son is sent "whence" to judge. The coming of the Lord frames the Christian hope. Christians live in expectation, awaiting the age of promise—the age in which Jesus Christ ushers in the fullness of God's kingdom.

During my teenage years in youth group, we used to be asked the question, "If the Lord were to return, what would he find you doing?" I don't know, but I wouldn't want to be at Disney World. Not that going to Disney World is sinful. I just don't want the Lord to find me on his return to judge the cosmos posing for a photo with Mickey Mouse. I don't want to be on Dumbo's little ride when the King of glory comes. I would much rather be found sharing the gospel with someone.

In reality Christians can live their lives in joy and in full assurance. They can eat, drink, sleep, and yes, even go to Disney World. The more important issue is not *where* you are when the Lord returns or even *what* you are doing. The question is, will he find you faithful? Will he find you as one who belongs to him through faith?

We don't know when Christ will return, but we do know *how* he will return. He will be coming in glory; he will be arrayed in splendor. If Isaiah saw God "sitting upon a throne, high and lifted up" (Isa. 6:1) with the train of his robe filling the temple, we, too, anticipate that day when the train of God's glory will fill the entire earth. From horizon to horizon, from the setting of the sun to its rising, the entire cosmos will instantaneously display the glory of God as the agent of creation, redemption, and judgment.

Christ is coming in glory, power, and majesty. He is also coming bodily. It is not a disembodied judge who is coming—it is Jesus, who will come bearing in his resurrection body the evidence of his suffering and atonement for our sins. As the Bible makes clear, there will be no one left in ignorance about the fact that judgment has now come (Matt. 16:27). John wrote, "Then I saw heaven opened, and behold, a white horse! The one sitting on it is called Faithful and True, and in righteousness he judges and makes war" (Rev. 19:11). This is where spiritual warfare ends:

> His eyes are like a flame of fire, and on his head are many diadems, and he has a name written that no one knows but himself. He is clothed in a robe dipped in blood, and the name by which he is called is The Word of God. And the armies of heaven, arrayed in fine linen, white and pure, were following him on white horses. From his mouth comes a sharp sword with which to strike down the nations, and he will rule them with a rod of iron. He will tread the winepress of the fury of the wrath of God the Almighty. On his robe and on his thigh he has a name written, King of kings and Lord of lords.
>
> Then I saw an angel standing in the sun, and with a loud voice he called to all the birds that fly directly overhead, "Come, gather for the great supper of God, to eat the flesh of kings, the flesh of captains, the flesh of mighty men, the flesh of horses and their riders, and the flesh of all men, both free and slave, both small and great." And I saw the beast and the kings of the earth with their armies gathered to make war against him who was sitting on the horse and against his army. (Rev. 19:12–19)

Christians can rest assured with *this* headline news. The King is coming! And the images here, lest they be overlooked, show a King coming with vengeance against his enemies.

This portrait of Jesus is not typically portrayed on Sunday school flannel graphs or at vacation Bible school. But the Holy Spirit uses this vivid and unmistakable language depicting Christ's majesty. The King is coming to claim his church, and he is coming to bring blessing and final consolation to his chosen people. He is coming to rescue his own from this evil age. And he is coming to execute judgment upon every single human being.

The Bible is very clear that on the last day Christ will separate the sheep from the goats. Christ's sheep will go into everlasting blessedness in heaven, and the goats will suffer everlasting torment in hell. We are living in a day in which there are many people trying to "air-condition hell." Even some evangelicals are attempting to minimize Scripture's teaching on hell—suggesting that it is not eternal torment; merely the annihilation of existence. This idea, however, does not fit with the biblical text.

One prominent theologian suggests that there is a hell but that those who are in hell merely have their personhood removed so that they are no longer truly human.[1] I find that clever, but I can't find that doctrine taught in the Bible. The impulse toward universalism is an effort to make sure that no one is ever in hell. Other liberal theologians try to temporalize hell so that it's a present reality of poverty or of suffering or of existential fear. But the Bible presents a very real hell of eternal conscious torment.

The cosmic display of God's holiness and mercy is coming. Anthony Hoekema has it exactly right: "The necessity of this judgment does not stem from there being any question about the destiny of the judged. That is already established."[2] Jesus himself made this clear by saying, "Whoever believes in him is not condemned, but whoever does not believe is condemned already, because he has not believed in the name of the only Son of God" (John 3:18). Those who have rejected the Son are condemned already. The condemnation has already been declared. So why must this great and terrible day of the Lord's judgment come?

First, this judgment will display God's sovereignty and his glory cosmically, so that every single human being—past, present, and future—comes face-to-face with the reality of the display of God's glory in the judgment of the Son.

Second, this judgment is necessary because, as Scripture makes clear, God will judge through Christ in such a way that there are gradients to his judgment by means of blessings for the redeemed and judgment upon those who did not believe.

Third, it is necessary that this judgment take place because there is a necessity for personal judgment. It's not just judgment against groups or nations. It is judgment of every single human being. A verdict will be declared for every single human being. For those who are in Christ, the verdict (by the imputed righteousness of Jesus Christ) will be unto salvation and eternal life. For those who are without Christ, the verdict will be damnation.

Perfect Justice

Human justice has always been and will always be limited. Judicial systems can put someone in prison or even put someone to death, but we cannot make things truly right. Perfect judgment that would establish righteousness and justice would not merely punish the wrongdoer but would give back life to the murdered and give back hope to the hopeless. It is not merely Christians and our awareness of sin that causes us to cry out for this kind of perfect justice. All creation is crying out.

Every single moment of pain cries out for the need of the judgment and the arrival of true justice. Indeed, Scripture testifies that true justice is coming. This great hope is missing from the horizon of so many Christians. Christ's judgment will be so perfect that all the judged—whether declared righteous through Christ or not—will agree with the righteousness of the judgment. Those who go to hell will fully know the rightfulness of that verdict, as will those who go to heaven because of what Christ has done on our behalf.

Perfect justice points to dual destinies—the sinful offender will receive exactly what is owed, and the offended Son of God will receive his glory. This judgment affirms the wrath of God, and if we flinch from speaking honestly about the wrath of God, then we can never speak honestly about the love of God. For the wrath of God is not his loss of temper. It is not an unrighteous anger. God's wrath is the appropriate and natural response of the Holy One to a rebellion against his perfect righteousness. Heaven and hell will bear witness to the perfect judgment of God.

These truths point again to the gospel, for no sinner in and of himself can find survival in this judgment. The only means of survival—the only means of acquittal or salvation—is the loving sacrifice of Christ, our defender and our judge. Christians must live with urgency because we understand that in this present age God will use us to snatch some from the evil one. The reality of the eschaton, the last days, reminds us of the urgency of sharing the gospel, because the eschaton goes hand in hand with the declaration of Jesus Christ among the nations. Our understanding of the future fuels our actions in the present; thus, missions and evangelism are eschatological activities—focused and fueled by the knowledge of Christ's coming.

The future was present in Christ, but the future is also present in the salvation of a single human being, a single sinner, who comes to faith in the Lord Jesus Christ. One who would be otherwise judged guilty and sent to hell will now be judged innocent—not because he or she is innocent but because that sinner is covered by the blood of the Lord Jesus Christ.

The fact that Christ is coming "whence to judge the quick and the dead" tells us that we are not going to have our best life now, nor should we look for it. For those who have their best life now are going to face a very different life in the age to come. We sing, we read Scripture, we share the gospel, we preach the Word against the backdrop of the coming kingdom. We can eat, drink, serve, and sleep with confidence only because we have assurance that we know the future. That future is Jesus Christ, and we are safe in him.

CHAPTER ELEVEN

THE HOLY SPIRIT

The Great Commission is, quite rightly, one of the texts of Scripture that Christians know best. Jesus told his disciples, "All authority in heaven and on earth has been given to me. Go therefore and make disciples of all nations, baptizing them in the name of the Father and of the Son and of the Holy Spirit, teaching them to observe all that I have commanded you. And behold, I am with you always, to the end of the age" (Matt. 28:18–20).

The Trinitarian form of Christian baptism—believers baptized in the name of the Father and of the Son and of the Holy Spirit, is one of the clearest and most familiar biblical testimonies to our triune God.

The Trinity is an unfathomable doctrine. No Christian can exhaust its meaning. At the same time no Christian can deny the Trinity, and this text helps us to understand why this is true. To know the one true God is to know him as Father, Son, and Holy Spirit. Where true Christianity is found, the affirmation of the Trinity is found.

One way to understand the doctrine of the Trinity is to consider that the doctrine emerged out of a need to affirm and explain that God is one—and yet also Father, Son, and Holy Spirit. Monotheism is basic and ascribed to God as revealed in both the Old and New Testaments. The Shema, the most central verse of Israel's faith, sets this truth majestically: "Hear, O Israel: The LORD our God, the LORD is one" (Deut. 6:4). That single verse could not be clearer. The entire Bible testifies that God is One.

Yet, at the same time and without the slightest consideration, the Bible also reveals and affirms the following propositions:

1. The Father is God.
2. The Son is God.
3. The Holy Spirit is God.

The doctrine of the Trinity is the faithful churches' way of holding all these revealed truths together, consistently and without confusion.

Looking back at the Great Commission, the pattern of Christian truth became crystal clear, even commanding baptism in the name of the Father and of the Son and of the Holy Spirit. As one of the most cherished hymns of the Christian faith elaborates, we praise God as "God in three persons, blessed Trinity."

In the seventh grade I entered into my first real theological controversy. It all began in the school cafeteria when a classmate began arguing about the gifts of the Holy Spirit, and she then began to question the legitimacy of my church and my theology. My classmate was caught up in the excitement of the charismatic movement, then resurgent on the American religious landscape.

I found myself arguing with my friend, but as I tried to frame my arguments, I came to an embarrassing realization—I didn't know enough about the Holy Spirit. As I later learned, I was not alone.

Many Christians fall shamelessly short in understanding the Holy Spirit, or the third person of the Trinity. When we confess together, "I believe in the Holy Spirit," we believe as Jesus Christ taught his church to believe. This phrase of the creed contains only six words, but these are six thundering words, revealing the mystery of God and reminding believers of our continual dependence on the Holy Spirit.

Despite the glories contained in this affirmation of the creed, so few of us today have any familiarity with the doctrine of the Holy Spirit, or what theologians call pneumatology. In some evangelical circles the Holy Spirit has faded into the background of our theological interests, leaving us with an anemic view of the Spirit, and subsequently, a deficient relationship with the third member of the Trinity. Jesus himself said, "Nevertheless, I tell you the truth: it is to your advantage that I go away, for if I do not go away, the Helper will not come to you. But if I go, I will send him to you" (John 16:7). Jesus told his disciples and all of us that to have the Spirit is actually better than to have the physical Christ in our presence. Astounding as this claim is, how often do believers think of the Spirit and his ministry? Do we really believe the words of Jesus found in John 16?

Our silence on the Spirit indicts our faith, dampens our worship, robs our churches, empties the gospel of its beauty, and fails to glory in the resplendent mystery of the Trinity. The reason for our silence, perhaps, stems from the innumerable misunderstandings and misappropriations of the doctrine of the Spirit. The endless debates and controversies have plagued Christian spirituality, causing many of us to shrink away from pneumatology altogether. Falling away and surrendering the ground of the truth of the Spirit, however, subverts our own spirituality and those who espouse false notions of the Spirit. We must not remain silent about this glorious doctrine. We must press head-on into the Scriptures and uncover the beauty that the Apostles' Creed affirms in this short article, "I believe in the Holy Spirit."

The Ministry of the Spirit: John 14–16

As Jesus prepared for his passion, he left his disciples with parting words of comfort. He knew the trouble and anguish in their souls as they came to terms with the reality that they would not be with their Master much longer. Jesus, therefore, instructed them on the ministry of the Spirit and the crucial role he would exert in their lives and ministry. In these three chapters, Jesus detailed the inexplicable joy of the gift of the Spirit, and our pervasive need for his coming (John 14–16). Jesus described the Spirit as the One who abides, the One who teaches, the One who testifies, and the One who bears truth.

The Spirit Who Abides

"And I will ask the Father, and he will give you another Helper, to be with you forever, even the Spirit of truth, whom the world cannot receive, because it neither sees him nor knows him. You know him, for he dwells with you and will be in you." (John 14:16–17)

No doubt, fear and panic flooded the disciples' hearts and minds as they listened to the Lord Jesus for the last time. They had followed him, loved him, and found their purpose in him. Indeed, Peter exclaimed, "Lord, to whom shall we go? You have the words of eternal life" (John 6:68). The disciples recognized, as we must, that without God we have no hope, no life. Without God we are dead and helpless. The fear of being left behind without Jesus gnawed away at the hearts of the disciples.

Jesus, however, promised not to leave them as orphans. The promise he gave to the disciples extends even to us. He uttered eternal words of comfort in saying that the Spirit would come. Not only would the Spirit come, but he would dwell with the disciples. Not only would he dwell with Christ's disciples, he would dwell *in* them. Jesus promised an unfathomable unity and inexplicable bond that will exist between the people of God and the Holy Spirit. The intimacy of the believer and the Spirit rises to the sacred language of *abiding*. The Spirit himself, the third member of the Trinity, *abides* in you, in me, and in all who belong to Jesus Christ through faith.

The Spirit's ministry of abiding in us restores all hope and secures us on the sure foundation of faith. Even when the Enemy assails us, he cannot overcome us because the Spirit dwells in us. As the Spirit abides in us, the full presence of God is among us and in us. The Holy Spirit, therefore, explains how the church survives and how the gospel spreads to the ends of the earth. The Spirit abiding in us explains how you and I can hear the words of the Bible not as the words of man but as God's revealed truth. Indeed, the Spirit's presence in you explains why you have life.

Jesus promised the Spirit as an abiding presence forever. Thus, the Spirit does not come in seasons of difficulty only. The Spirit does not flee from you when you continually struggle with sin. His presence in you does not hinge upon your obedience or effort. His presence in you rests upon the infinite grace and love of God for you. God knows that without the Spirit, we will perish. He promises the Spirit, therefore, to dwell intimately *in* us, forever.

The Spirit Who Teaches

> But the Helper, the Holy Spirit, whom the Father will send in my name, he will teach you all things and bring to your remembrance all that I have said to you. (John 14:26)

As the disciples came to terms with the coming physical absence of Jesus, they no doubt felt the pain of losing their beloved teacher. When Jesus taught, he taught as one with authority (Matt. 7:29). Indeed, Jesus did not merely come and proclaim the Word of the Lord; he reigned as Lord of the Word. His teaching cast out demons, gave life to the dead, proclaimed the present and coming kingdom, and revealed the true glories of the Scriptures. As Peter confessed above, the words that came from Jesus' lips were nothing less than the words of life.

Now the disciples began to understand that Jesus was going to be with the Father. Jesus, however, promised the coming of the Spirit as one who will not only abide, but *teach*. The Spirit of God will come upon all those who believe in Christ and teach us *all things* and bring to our minds the inspired Word of God. Jesus ensured that his disciples would not suffer the loss of his teaching. He ensured its preaching through the power and indwelling of the Holy Spirit in all God's people.

The teaching ministry of the Spirit must bring great comfort to us and radically transform the way we approach the Scriptures. Do you come to God's Word in humble prayer, asking the Spirit to guide you, teach you, and direct your thoughts? Do you realize the glorious truth Christ here proclaims to you: that the Spirit of God dwells in you to teach you the things of God? The Spirit, furthermore, teaches all the people of God through the Word and through the preaching of the Word. This means that the Spirit brings us together in covenant community to learn together as one people of God.

We need the Spirit, therefore, in our own private time in the Word, praying for his presence to instruct us and lead us. We also must pray for the Spirit to teach the church. He instructs all God's people through the ministry of the Word. Without him our own understanding of God would fail and the church itself would crumble under the weight of false teaching. The Spirit, through his teaching ministry, preserves and protects each individual believer as well as ensures the doctrinal purity of the whole body of Christ.

The Bible is itself the gift of the Holy Spirit, and every single word of Scripture is inspired of God. Peter affirmed this truth when he, led by the Holy Spirit, wrote: "For no prophecy was ever produced by the will of man, but men spoke from God as they were carried along by the Holy Spirit" (2 Peter 1:21). Carried along by the Holy Spirit! And the promise of God is that the very Holy Spirit who gave us the holy Scriptures enables Christians to read and to understand the Bible today. The Bible is a living Word because it is the Word of God, "living and active, sharper than any two-edged sword, piercing to the division of soul and of spirit, of joints and of marrow, and discerning the thoughts and intentions of the heart" (Heb. 4:12).

The Holy Spirit gave us the Scriptures, opens our eyes to see the Scriptures, and opens our hearts to believe God's Word. The Holy Spirit empowers the preaching of the Word and ensures that it never returns void (Isa. 55:11).

The Spirit Who Testifies

> But when the Helper comes, whom I will send to you from the Father, the Spirit of truth, who proceeds from the Father, he will bear witness about me. And you also will bear witness, because you have been with me from the beginning. (John 15:26–27)

A wonderful mystery surrounds this passage as Jesus revealed an order of authority in the Trinity. The order of authority in no way postulates a hierarchy of divinity and power within the Trinity. Each member of the Trinity is consubstantial, equal in divinity and power, very God of very God. The Bible, however, also presents us with the mystery of the triune God, a glorious mystery in which all in Christ will glory forever and ever. In these verses from John, Jesus revealed that the Spirit will come and not bear witness of himself, but of Christ.

This essential truth explains why we do not speak of the Holy Spirit with the same language and knowledge we do about the Father and the Son. The Holy Spirit comes to bear witness and testify to the person and work of Christ. The Holy Spirit, therefore, exalts the Son and testifies to his accomplished work at Calvary. This amounts to an important reality check for churches across the world: Where you find the Spirit of God present, you do not find so much testimony *about* the Holy Spirit as you find a testimony about Christ. Where you find, therefore, a bold, biblical, urgent, accurate, enthusiastic, joyful, and life-changing testimony of Christ, you can rest assured that the Holy Spirit is vibrantly at work.

This truth protects us from the errors that plague so many churches that place an unbiblical emphasis on the Holy Spirit. The Spirit becomes the center of their faith. The Spirit consumes their thoughts as they try to arouse manifestations of the Spirit in their own lives and congregations. Jesus, however, reminded his disciples what the testimony the Spirit will bring: a testimony about Jesus, exalting Christ, and pointing us to the hope we have in union with him.

The Spirit Who Bears Truth

> When the Spirit of truth comes, he will guide you into all the truth, for he will not speak on his own authority, but whatever he hears he will speak, and he will declare to you the things that are to come. He will glorify me, for he will take what is mine and declare it to you. (John 16:13–14)

Finally, we learn from Jesus that the Spirit comes to bear the truth. In fact, this passage tells us that the Spirit *is truth*. He not only comes to bear witness to the truth, he comes as truth. The truth, therefore, comes and dwells in and among God's people. Christ could claim his departure benefited the disciples only because the Spirit would dwell in God's people and proclaim the truth of God inwardly in his people.

Christians must take comfort from the Spirit of truth that dwells in them. We live in a post-truth age, an age that all but denies the existence of any absolute truth. The reality of our cultural context will naturally inform our evangelistic strategies. We must not, however, think that the post-truth age we live in has not had a residual effect on our own perceptions of reality and truth. The Holy Spirit does not deliver contradictory testimony in God's people. He testifies to *the* truth. At times the truth he bears brings about conviction of our own actions and conduct. Sometimes, the truth he proclaims calls us to embark on an arduous course of action. Sometimes, the truth can be very difficult to confront. We must, however, know that the Spirit in us is the Spirit of truth. He will bear witness to the truth requiring a response to his testimony. The Holy Spirit calls us to the truth of God and his will for our lives. As he does this, Christians must remember that the truth will set you free (John 8:32).

Life in the Spirit

Jesus' words to his disciples recorded in John 14–16 reveal the ministry of the Holy Spirit that each and every believer will experience in their walk with Christ. The Bible, however, presses the realities of the Spirit's ministries into our personal lives. The Bible calls us to walk by the Spirit (Gal. 5:16), that our lives must be led by the Spirit (Rom. 8:14). It is necessary, therefore, in light of the Spirit's ministry, to explore the relationship believers must have with the Spirit. This relationship informs how we might live a life that exalts Christ, kills sin, and perseveres till the end.

Putting to Death the Deeds of the Body

So then, brothers, we are debtors, not to the flesh, to live according to the flesh. For if you live according to the flesh you will die, but if by the Spirit you put to death the deeds of the body, you will live. (Rom. 8:12–13)

Romans 8 concludes the glorious presentation of Paul's gospel. Indeed, in verse 1, Paul reveals the wonderful, life-giving truth that there is no condemnation for those who are in Christ Jesus. Christ took the condemnation of the law upon himself, and God, through our faith in Christ, credits the righteousness of Jesus to us in full. Thus, faith in Christ not only cleanses us from our sin, but gives us the complete righteousness of Jesus Christ. That is why there is no condemnation for those who are in Christ Jesus.

The glory of the great exchange—Christ taking your sin upon himself and crediting his righteousness to you—does not, however, allow for a life of continual, unrepentant sin. This false notion is known as antinomianism. If Christians live free from the requirements of the law through Christ, then may a Christian live as he or she wishes? Paul asked a similar question at the beginning of Romans 6, where he responded with a resounding, "By no means!" Paul informed Christians that their lives must now be lived in the Spirit (Rom. 8). We must set our minds on things that are above (Col. 3:2). Christians must not set their minds on the flesh, "for to set the mind on the flesh is death, but to set the mind on the Spirit is life and peace" (Rom. 8:6). Christians, therefore, must kill sin and pursue holiness.

How can Christians hope to live holy lives in the midst of a sinful world, with Satan continually prowling around, looking for someone to devour? How can Christians pursue Christlikeness while beset with indwelling sin and living in a body of flesh? Paul answered this question in Romans 8:12–13. He exclaimed that, by nature of our union with Christ, we must not live according to the flesh. Paul warned that if we continue to live according to the flesh, we will prove we never belonged to Christ and will die. If, however, we put to death the deeds of the body *by the Spirit*, we will live.

The inclusion of "by the Spirit" is not just a passing reference. Paul, under the influence of the Spirit himself, included this vital component of Christian sanctification. We cannot hope to put sin to death if we do not depend upon the power of the Spirit. We will fail every test, give way to every temptation, and falter before our ancient foe unless we cry out for the Spirit to empower us, guide us, and fill us with his strength to help us endure. The ministry of the Spirit—his abiding, teaching, testifying, and truth-bearing ministry—must not remain a theological concept only believed in the mind. Our hearts also need to experience it.

Christians must cultivate this relationship with the Spirit and pray to him. Believers in Jesus Christ must recognize that without the Spirit all hope of sanctification and perseverance diminishes. Do you pray to the Spirit every day and ask him to aid you in your fight against sin? Do you cry out, as David did, "Take not your Holy Spirit from me"? (Ps. 51:11). The Bible teaches our desperate need for the Spirit and his continual ministry in our lives. Do you earnestly pray for him to abide in you in power, teach in truth, and testify to the glory of Christ? Brothers and sisters, you cannot kill sin without the ministry of the Spirit. I ask, therefore, are you desperate for him? Christ grants the Spirit to his people for a splendid purpose. He does not send the Spirit, the third member of the Trinity, for anything less than God's eternal purposes for you and for his church. Jesus knows our need for the Spirit. Do you?

Bearing the Fruit of the Spirit

> But I say, walk by the Spirit, and you will not gratify the desires of the flesh. . . . But the fruit of the Spirit is love, joy, peace, patience, kindness, goodness, faithfulness, gentleness, self-control. (Gal. 5:16, 22–23)

Putting to death the deeds of the body necessarily requires a bearing of the fruit of the Spirit. Indeed, Paul said, "For the one who sows to his own flesh will from the flesh reap corruption, but the one who sows to the Spirit will from the Spirit reap eternal life" (Gal. 6:8). The Christian life, therefore, sows to the Spirit, which reaps not only a harvest free from the poison of sin but also bears the fruit of the Spirit.

Anyone not bearing the fruit of the Spirit does not belong to Christ. Our life in the Spirit means that the virtues of godliness grow and manifest themselves in our daily lives. As we kill sin by the power of the Spirit, we also, by walking with the Spirit, display the fruit of godliness and the very character of the Spirit himself. As we walk by the Spirit, the depth of our love, the fullness of our joy, the solidity of our peace, the lengths of our patience, the exuberance of our kindness, the breadth of our goodness, the greatness of our faithfulness, the meekness of our gentleness, and the sacrifice of our self-control all flourish and bear a glorious harvest sweet to others and delightful to God. Brothers and sisters, your walk with the Spirit is meant to be a fruitful, powerful, and joyful walk.

The cultivation of Christian virtue can only be accomplished through the ministry of the Spirit in our lives. You, however, must seek him and walk with him. You must pursue God in his Word, and press in toward vibrant community and fellow-ship with God's people. You must pray to God and sow to your relationship with him. Your intimacy with the Spirit produces a harvest that the world cannot help but notice. I love Acts 4:13, where the Jewish leaders are astounded at Peter and John. It says, "Now when they saw the boldness of Peter and John, and perceived that they were uneducated, common men, they were astonished. *And they recognized that they had been with Jesus.*" Indeed, the world will know the depth of your communion with God. The world will recognize those who walk intimately with the Spirit. All God's people have benefited greatly from saints who traversed the sweetest paths of felicity with the Spirit, long-ing to bear his virtue and glory in their lives.

I encourage you, therefore, to walk by the Spirit. *Know* him and meet with him daily in the Word and through the power of your local church and fellowship. Depend upon the Spirit to bear his fruit in your life. Galatians 5:16 comes, not as empty words, but as a *promise* of God. *If* you walk by the Spirit, *you will not* gratify the desires of the flesh. *If* you sow to the Spirit, *you will reap* from the Spirit eternal life.

Conclusion

"I believe in the Holy Spirit." Never have six short words con-fessed something so magnificent, glorious, powerful, and beautiful. This confession asserts nothing less than the power that indwells every believer of Jesus Christ. This confession affirms the truth of the One who abides in us, teaches us, testi-fies to Christ, and bears the fullness of God's truth in our lives. This confession delineates the indescribable need each and every one of God's people have for the ministry of the Spirit in their lives. This confession also encompasses the splendid promises of God contained in the gift of the Spirit. I began this chapter with the lamentable state of pneumatology in contemporary evangelical circles. I pray that God's Word and the truths outlined in the Apostles' Creed will call us to repentance and to a new, vibrant, and fruitful relationship with the Spirit of God, the Spirit who dwells in us and who has sealed us forever in the eternal promises of the triune God.

CHAPTER TWELVE

THE HOLY CATHOLIC CHURCH AND THE COMMUNION OF SAINTS

The Apostles' Creed now pivots from affirmations about God to the identity and character of God's people. As the creed affirms a belief in the church—holy and catholic (universal)—it postulates a conviction in an ecclesial, covenantal, and eternal community of the people of God. In so doing, the creed dispels any notion of individualistic Christianity. The creed, therefore, places an emphasis not on *me* but *we*. Not on *I* but *us*.

The very first day I was a student at Southern Seminary, I sat down in a classroom to begin a course on church history. There I was, in Norton Hall 195, when Timothy George, a bearded church historian, entered the room. He was freshly minted with a doctorate from Harvard, and I was ready to learn church history. I wasn't ready for what he said. He looked out at us, surveyed the room, and said, "My task is to inform you that there was someone between Jesus and your grandmother and then to convince you that it matters." It struck me like a bullet, because he made the argument so unforgettably. Yes, there are so many believers and so many centuries between Jesus and my grandmother—and they *do* matter.

Contemporary Christianity often fails to grasp the depths of the creed's affirmation and the importance of the long, unbroken line of communion Christians share as members of Christ's church. The horizon of American Christianity continues to recede as it embraces the rugged ethos of American individualism. The ethic of personal autonomy shapes the minds, expectations, and worldviews of most Americans. This ethic, regrettably, permeates throughout many evangelical churches. We have no place in our thinking of what it means to believe in the church and the communion of saints. Indeed, the stereotypical American church has devolved into a voluntary association, no different from a local club or service organization. American ecclesiology often capitulates to a spiritual "cafeteria" designed to meet preferential wants rather than gather together the people of God for Christ-exalting community and worship. The American church has been relegated to a consumer good rather than the body of the risen King of the universe.

The Apostles' Creed, however, will not permit any deficient view of the church of Jesus Christ. The Apostles' Creed enshrines a robust and biblical ecclesiology and places within its glorious confession an unshakable affirmation of the church. The wisdom of the church fathers continues to cascade throughout the creed as they insist upon a doctrine of the church alongside affirmations of the Trinity, the atonement, and the mysterious union of the deity and humanity of Jesus Christ. For Christians, therefore, a right understanding of theology must include a clear and comprehensive ecclesiology—the doctrine of the church.

Regrettably, however, an anemic ecclesiology inevitably produces an anemic church. We must, therefore, recapture in our theology what Christians have understood as essential to the Christian faith. Embedded in the affirmation of our belief in the church is nothing less than our identity. To understand, however, the riches encapsulated in the doctrine of the church, we must first turn to its foundation described to us in Matthew 16.

The Foundation of the Church: Peter's Confession in Matthew 16

In each of the Gospels, a paradigmatic shift occurs when Jesus asked his disciples what *they* thought about his identity. Everything changed when Jesus turned from asking what other people were saying about him to asking his disciples, "But what do you say?"

Now when Jesus came into the district of Caesarea Philippi, he asked his disciples, "Who do people say that the Son of Man is?" And they said, "Some say John the Baptist, others say Elijah, and others Jeremiah or one of the prophets." He said to them, "But who do you say that I am?" Simon Peter replied, "You are the Christ, the Son of the living God." And Jesus answered him, "Blessed are you, Simon Bar-Jonah! For flesh and blood has not revealed this to you, but my Father who is in heaven. And I tell you, you are Peter, and on this rock I will build my church, and the gates of hell shall not prevail against it. I will give you the keys of the kingdom of heaven, and whatever you bind on earth shall be bound in heaven, and whatever you loose on earth shall be loosed in heaven." (Matt. 16:13–19)

In these verses Peter confessed the identity of Jesus Christ. Peter identified Jesus as more than a prophet or a mere teacher. Peter confessed that Jesus is none other than the Son of God and the Messiah, the promised seed of the woman, which takes us back all the way to Genesis 3. Peter did not come to his conclusion merely through theological reflection, however. God the Father, by his grace, revealed the identity of his Son to Peter and enabled him to proclaim the true nature of the One who stood before him.

After Peter's answer Jesus announced a message that would change the course of the entire world and of all human history. Jesus said that upon Peter's words, he would build his church. This text demonstrates four elements that make up the ontology of Jesus' bride. Jesus revealed that his church is to be founded upon a confession, on truth, in power, and with authority.

Founded upon a Confession

Jesus built his church upon Peter's *confession*. These days, most Americans use the word *confess* to mean making an admission of wrongdoing. But, as we have seen, to confess the faith is to hold and to defend the faith in public—to confess the faith with the saints is to confess the faith with the witness of all true Christians throughout the ages. This is why creeds are referred to as confessions of faith—we confess the faith *together*. Peter confessed that in Christ lay all the hopes of Israel. In Christ are fulfilled all the expectations for salvation the world has longed for and eagerly awaited. Peter proclaimed the divinity of Jesus, God incarnate, Immanuel. In just a few words, Peter affirmed the ground-breaking, earth-shattering truth that changed the course of human history.

The effects of Peter's confession did not end there. Jesus responded by saying that on Peter he would build his church. In essence Jesus proclaimed that his body would be built upon the words as spoken by Peter. Where Peter's confession is found, the church is found. Where that confession is proclaimed, you will find the communion of saints. Thus, Peter's confession established the faith of the church of God and how any may find entrance into that covenant community. Entrance into the people of God begins with a confession of Jesus Christ as Lord, Son of the living God. All who make that confession, by God's grace, become his people and unite themselves to Christ and to Christ's body, the church. When sinners confess the truth that Peter proclaimed (Matt. 16) and obey Christ in baptism, they come into the church forever. They are, from that point on, never alone.

Founded on Truth

Jesus does not build his church upon any mere confession of men. No, he builds his bride on lasting and eternal truth. Indeed, Paul reminded us that the church stands as the pillar of truth in a world twisted by lies and deceit (1 Tim. 3:15). Thus, a true and right confession of Christ becomes a central part of what it means to be the church.

Where the church fails to declare the truth, it forfeits its status as a true church. When churches capitulate and compromise the truth, they betray their status as part of God's people. The culture beckons us to come and take up modern and rational sensibilities. The call to jettison the truths of the gospel tempts God's people in every corner of the globe. Matthew 16, however, will not allow God's people to separate themselves from God's truth. The church proclaims the truth, holds to the truth, and embodies the truth, even unto death. Without the truth proclaimed in Matthew 16, humanity possesses no hope. Thus, the people of God stand upon Peter's confession of the truth, like a mighty rock that no wave of dissent can overcome. The contemporary church especially must heed the implications of Peter's confession. We must never depart from the truth. As Paul wrote to Timothy, the church bears the perpetual responsibility to guard the deposit entrusted to it (2 Tim. 1:14). As noted earlier, Jude warned all believers that the church must contend and defend the faith *"once for all delivered to the saints"* (Jude 1:3).

Founded in Power

Jesus also founded his church in power. He said that not even the gates of hell will prevail against his people. More than anything else, this means that Christians cannot be separated from Christ, even by death. Death itself cannot sever us from Christ and his saving power. Though Christians suffer death, we die safely. Why? Because Christ has united his people to himself in his body, the church. The church, therefore, unlike anything on earth, will be the only institution to transcend the ages. Nothing less than the eternal blood of Christ purchased the church, his bride, forever and ever. This is the power of the church: that even hell and all its powers will never prevail because the church belongs to Christ.

The church's power lies not in a military government or in

any political party. The church does not derive power from the culture or economic might. No, the church's power is a spiritual power grounded in the power of the gospel. The church, therefore, must never live in fear but in hope, for Christ gave his people power even over the grave. Death comes, but Christ will return. Death will not be able to hold onto Jesus' bride. Christ has defeated death once for all, and those who are in Christ will know everlasting life. The truth embedded in Peter's confession stands like an insurmountable mountain that all the forces of darkness combined cannot overcome.

Founded with Authority

Finally, Jesus, upon Peter's confession, granted authority to the church. Jesus told his disciples, "I will give you the keys of the kingdom of heaven, and whatever you bind on earth shall be bound in heaven, and whatever you loose on earth shall be loosed in heaven" (Matt. 16:19). Though the language of "binding" and "loosing" may seem strange to us, Jesus' disciples would have immediately grasped Jesus' declaration. Jewish rabbis would stand at the city gates and carry out the duty of binding and loosing. The rabbis would adjudicate issues brought by the people. They would look to the Scriptures and reason from them conclusions that were understood to be binding or loosing. The Scriptures bound or loosed the people. Now, Jesus declared, "I grant this power to the church." This power belongs to Christ alone, but now, he delegates this power to his people. Jesus bestowed awesome responsibility to the church. The church must now steward this power and authority for God's glory, handling all cases that rise in the church, great and small, on the basis of God's revelation in Scripture.

The church, which exists by God's authority, was established by Jesus Christ, is empowered by the Holy Spirit, and is fully authorized to preach the Word of God and to decide matters great and small by interpreting and applying the Scriptures. This is the power of the keys—and the keys are held by the church—wherever the church is found.

Conclusion

Peter's confession, though just a few words in length, thunders through the ages: "You are the Christ, the Son of the living God." Upon these words, which Peter spoke only by the revelation and grace of God, Jesus established his church. Jesus, therefore, revealed that his church builds upon and only upon the confession of Jesus as Lord and the Son of God. This confession, furthermore, insists that the church must be built upon truth and hold fast to the truth of the gospel. Jesus also endowed his bride with an insurmountable power—a power that Satan himself cannot overturn even by death. Finally, Jesus granted his church authority here on earth to carry out its God-given duties and to shine the light of Christ to a lost and dying world.

The Identity of the Church

Matthew 16 describes the *establishment* of the church. We must not, however, stop there. Understanding the establishment of the church lays the necessary foundation upon which we can build. We now turn to understand the identity of the church. The story of the church does not end with Peter's confession. It does not even end in Acts 28. The church presses on into the annals of history. In every subsequent century, the church has continued to unfold its identity and the essential marks of a church. Four specific marks have been noted and cherished throughout the history of the church for the last twenty centuries. The church is identified as one, holy, universal (catholic), and apostolic. These identifying marks have been lost in contemporary ecclesiology and must be recaptured if the church is to again embody and live out its identity as the people of God.

One

The idea of one church seems laughable in an age of thousands of denominations. How can any claim to see the church when all Christianity looks like are churches? Regardless of how impossible it seems to affirm that the church is one, we must nevertheless hold to the oneness of the church. The church represents the *one* people of God. This unity must be seen in relation to a spiritual unity, not an institutional unity.

At times throughout the history of the church, some have tried to build an institutional unity of the church. The results ended with a capitulation of truth. Thus, even in our ecclesiology, the doctrine of sin rears its head. Though the church exists as a divine institution, sinful humans clothed in their full humanity operate the church and execute its function. This means disagreements arise, even on fundamental matters or organizational life. We do, however, know this: wherever the confession "Jesus is Lord" is found and the gospel is affirmed, there is a oneness there that testifies to the invisible unity that exists between all God's people and that will only be realized upon Christ's return. Even now, there is one people of God, one church, one bride. This recognition should dispel any notions of racial, ethnic, or cultural supremacy. All Christians, throughout all human history and around the entire globe, represent the *one* people of God—the church.

Christians have sometimes divided wrongly, but the important thing to keep in mind is that the true unity of the church is, in this age, not institutional but theological. When the Scripture is rightly preached and the gospel is cherished, there is the church. When Jesus Christ is confessed as Lord and justification by faith alone is preached—there is the church.

Denominations result whenever deep convictions and religious freedom are found. Under religious liberty Christians are free to establish congregations and denominations by convictions.

One day, when Jesus Christ comes to claim his church, we will know a true and eternal institutional unity—we will all be together in Christ. There will be no Baptist or Methodist or Presbyterian or Lutheran or Anglican congregations in heaven—only the one people of God unified forever in truth.

The New Testament speaks of the church as the entire body of Christ, everywhere and through all ages. But the primary use of the word in the New Testament refers to visible congregations—each fully empowered to preach the gospel and to do the work of the ministry. Though many, the church is *one* under the lordship of Christ.

Holy

On the night of his betrayal, Jesus prayed his high priestly prayer recorded in John 17. In his prayer for the church, Jesus asked the Father to sanctify his people. Jesus revealed the longing of his heart for his people: that we be a sanctified people, a holy people, devoted to God and his Word. God's people, therefore, ought to be a holy people. In his prayer Jesus repeatedly made a clear distinction between the church and the world. The supreme distinguishing mark of God's people shines through their holiness, their separation from the world. This does not mean a physical separation. The holiness of the church comes through a qualitative difference from the rest of the world. The church should embody the spirit of Christ and brilliantly display his resplendent glory to a dark, dying world. The lives of God's people are radically different because they serve a new Master and find themselves constrained by a new love and affection.

This holiness does not arise out of an intrinsic character in our own nature. The holiness we must exemplify, like our righteousness, comes from the Lord himself. We cannot hope to be holy by our own merit. We rise to holiness only by the empowering work of Christ and the grace of God. Thus, the church must ache and long for the Spirit to fill it and its people with new hearts and affections set on the will of God. The church must not view striving for holiness through dependence as a mere ideal but as a daily duty. God has called his people to be holy, for he himself is holy (Lev. 11:44; 1 Peter 1:16). Where the church is found, therefore, it had better be found holy.

Universal

The temptation arises, as we confess the Apostles' Creed, to skip over the designation *catholic*. Confusion surrounds this word, and some may think they, in reciting this line, are affirming *Roman* Catholicism or the rule of the pope. But that is not what the word *catholic* affirms. We need to reclaim the word and confess it boldly and with joy. The word *catholic* here simply means universal. Thus, wherever the church is found, it is the same church. We believe, therefore, in Christianity, not in "Christianities"; we believe in the gospel, not in "gospels."

This notion of a universal church does not dispense with the rule and affirmation of the local church. Indeed, the book of Acts details the story of a local church in Jerusalem and the founding of other local churches around the ancient world. In fact, a proper ecclesiology particularly emphasizes the fact that every local church is an embassy of the eschatological kingdom. As D. A. Carson explained:

> Each local church is not seen primarily as one member parallel to a lot of other member churches, together constituting one body, one church; nor is each local church seen as the body of Christ parallel to other earthly churches that are also the body of Christ—as if Christ had many bodies. Rather, each church is the full manifestation in space and time of the one, true, heavenly, eschatological, new covenant church. Local churches should see themselves as outcroppings of heaven, analogies of "the Jerusalem that is above," indeed colonies of the new Jerusalem, providing on earth a corporate and visible expression of "the glorious freedom of the children of God."[1]

Thus, to believe in the universality of the church affirms a fundamental belief in the authority of the local congregation as well as an expectation of being united to Christ with all believers throughout the ages in the new heavens and the new earth. To confess "I believe in the holy catholic [universal] Church" confesses the universal nature of the church revealed in every local congregation that espouses and holds fast to the gospel *and* the expectation of a day when the *entire* universal church will join together at the wedding supper of the Lamb.

Apostolic

Finally, the identity of the church must flow from an apostolic proclamation. When we claim apostolicity as an identity of the church, we do not literally mean that there is a line of authoritative teachers that can be traced unbroken throughout Christian history. We do not mean that the office of apostle continues in the church today. The affirmation of apostolicity can be seen in Paul's words: "You then, my child, be strengthened by the grace that is in Christ Jesus, and what you have heard from me in the presence of many witnesses entrust to faithful men, who will be able to teach others also" (2 Tim. 2:1–2). Paul instructed his disciple Timothy to make disciples who, in time, make disciples. Timothy must hand down what he learned from the apostle Paul to faithful teachers who can teach others also. In essence Paul longed for a long line of godly and faithful teachers through whom the church would be fed and taught, as if from Christ himself.

Two thousand years after Paul lived, our hope should ever be that we proclaim the same gospel Paul taught and handed down to Timothy. We must be a church founded upon the apostolic teaching and proclamation. The church inherited the instructions and teaching of Christ from the apostles who followed and learned from Jesus. To be identified as a church, therefore, means that you teach all that the apostles taught. This identity means that we guard the deposit entrusted to us and pass it down to faithful men and women who will teach others also. The designation *apostolic*, therefore, must exemplify the character and constitution of the church and proclaim a wholly truthful and faithful apostolic message.

The Communion of Saints

The creed naturally flows from a belief in the holy catholic Church to a confession of the communion of saints. The holy catholic

Church *is* a communion of saints. The creed, therefore, derides any notion of individualism or a "go-it-alone" Christianity. The creed calls all Christians to recognize their new identity as eternal members of the eternal family of the eternal God. Churches across America must recapture a biblical vision of the felicitous bonds that unite each and every believer together in a glorious communion that extends throughout all the ages and has been secured by nothing less than the blood of Jesus Christ.

Hebrews 12—a Great Cloud of Witnesses

Hebrews 12 reveals the indescribable depths and riches of the communion that exists between Christ's people.

> Therefore, since we are surrounded by so great a cloud of witnesses, let us also lay aside every weight, and sin which clings so closely, and let us run with endurance the race that is set before us, looking to Jesus, the founder and perfecter of our faith, who for the joy that was set before him endured the cross, despising the shame, and is seated at the right hand of the throne of God. (vv. 1–2)

An invisible cloud of brothers and sisters who have gone before us presently surrounds all of us. The cloud of saints witnesses to the faithfulness of God and to the promised celestial gathering of all God's people. They cheer us on to run, as the people of God. They beckon us to press on so that we may join their eternal throng and their sweet, sinless gathering.

The author of Hebrews continued a few verses later, saying,

> For you have not come to what may be touched, a blazing fire and darkness and gloom and a tempest and the sound of a

trumpet and a voice whose words made the hearers beg that no further messages be spoken to them. For they could not endure the order that was given, "If even a beast touches the mountain, it shall be stoned." Indeed, so terrifying was the sight that Moses said, "I tremble with fear." But you have come to Mount Zion and to the city of the living God, the heavenly Jerusalem, and to innumerable angels in festal gathering, and to the assembly of the firstborn who are enrolled in heaven, and to God, the judge of all, and to the spirits of the righteous made perfect, and to Jesus, the mediator of a new covenant, and to the sprinkled blood that speaks a better word than the blood of Abel. (vv. 18–24)

The author of Hebrews revealed the glory of the new covenant. We no longer come, as Old Testament believers did, to a mountain that we cannot touch as it is consumed with the fire of God's holiness and glory. Instead, in Christ, we come to Mount Zion, to God's city. We come not as visitors or passersby. No! We come as *citizens* of that celestial city. We come to join in song with that great cloud of witnesses and proclaim the excellencies of him who we now see face-to-face.

Hebrews reveals this to the church so that God's people, today, can live with unshakable confidence in the day to come. If this is our destiny as God's people, then we must believe in the communion of saints and live like we believe it! As the body of Christ, we must today live like a community of pilgrims, pressing on toward that final, perfect, and cosmic union of all God's people from every age, gathered together to witness the dawning of the new eternal kingdom.

Scripture does not identify only special clans of believers, now dead, who have attained any special status. All Christians are made saints—holy ones—in and by Christ. Christians are not to pray to saints or to ask the saints for prayer. Christ is our sole sufficient Mediator and Intercessor as our Great High Priest. But we draw real encouragement and real courage from the communion of the saints—both those alive on earth and those alive in Christ in the great host of witnesses.

One Church, in Christ

Christ's people live by the Word of God. Our true unity is in Christ and in the holy Scriptures—God's inerrant and infallible Word. And yet, we are not embarrassed or reluctant to learn from Christians who have gone before us preaching the Word of God and teaching the Christian faith.

As a blood-bought people, we learn how to read and consider great teachers and preachers throughout the history of the church. Mature Christians learn to read with discernment, care, and gratitude. We learn much from theologians in the past, such as Augustine (AD 354–430), and from the creeds produced by the early church councils as the right confession of Christ and the doctrine of the Trinity were hammered out. We engage the theologians and doctrinal considerations of every age, with the Bible as our sure guide and standard of faith.

We stand in the faith of the great Reformers in the sixteenth century and with the faith of the Reformation, summarized formally in the "Five *Solas*": *Sola Fide, Sola Gratia, Sola Christus, Sola Scriptura, Soli Deo Gloria*—faith alone, grace alone, Christ alone, Scripture alone, to the glory of God alone.

We gladly learn from the Puritans and from titans of the faith like Jonathan Edwards and Charles Spurgeon. We have a rich ancestry of theology and Christian teaching. This, too, is one of the gifts of the communion of saints. We are a church made courageous by the examples of countless ministers and martyrs who have gone before us. The communion of the saints reminds us that we are with them—together forever in Christ's church.

The Danger of "I"

A belief in the holy catholic Church and the communion of saints simultaneously rejects the rugged individualism that has infested American evangelicalism. To be sure, admittance into Christ's church comes through an individual profession of faith and an individual confession of the truths of the gospel. We must give individual testimony to his transforming effect on our lives.

That must not, however, give rise to the notion that we go it alone. We are never alone. The thought that we can walk this Christian life alone carries with it a toxicity and poison that has deeply encumbered the American church. This individualism not only betrays the church, it betrays the gospel. It insinuates that the gospel is about God saving people without pointing to a bigger story of God creating *a people*. From the Old Testament to the New, the covenants, God's purposes, indeed the very creation of the world, all point to God's design of creating a people—a people that will be made up of every tribe, tongue, and nation. By God's grace we come through faith to Christ and thereby stand united as the whole people of God.

When we make this walk of faith about "me," we forsake the fullness of the gospel. The gospel does not allow us to boil down its glory to a story about "I" and "me." The story of the gospel encompasses in resplendent unity all the people of God, together, as one people. The gospel is God's story as he, through Christ, made a people for his pleasure. God's people, therefore, never find themselves alone. The sinner who comes to faith in a hotel room reading a New Testament is not alone. The saint dying as a martyr for the faith does not die alone. The missionary taking the gospel to the far reaches of the globe does not go alone. At the moment of our death, if we are in Christ, we are not alone. Brothers and sisters, we are never alone!

A great tragedy has besieged so many in this generation. Few Christians live today who cannot tell their story without telling the church's story as well. A failure of true fellowship has robbed believers across this nation of the riches of all that is contained in the Apostles' Creed on the subject. If you were asked to tell about your testimony and Christian walk, how central would the church be to your story?

We must repent from our anemic ecclesiology and embrace all that the Apostles' Creed espouses in the belief of the holy catholic Church and the communion of saints. Believers must embrace their identity as a *people* bought with the blood of Christ. We must seek to live as those who will one day spend all eternity together, clothed in the righteousness of Christ, singing together as one people the glories of our God. We must say, as Paul said, that we should have "the same mind, having the same love, being in full accord and of one mind. Do nothing from selfish ambition or conceit, but in humility count others more significant than yourselves. Let each of you look not only to his own interests, but also to the interests of others. Have this mind among yourselves, which is yours in Christ Jesus" (Phil. 2:2–5). Indeed, may we have the mind of Christ, who descended from his throne to ransom for himself a people, a church, a communion of saints for all eternity.

CHAPTER THIRTEEN

THE FORGIVENESS
OF SINS

The next phrase of the Apostles' Creed introduces, for the first time, something to confess about humanity. The creed, up to this point, declared the glorious work of the triune God, the splendor and scandal of Christ's ministry, the universal and sovereign reign of the resurrected Christ, the promise of future judgment, and the establishment of the church. Now, however, the creed turns to the character of mankind. Humanity finally shows up, and we show up as sinners.

The creed affirms the biblical truth of the sinfulness of mankind and God's impending judgment on sin and sinners who have rebelled against his holy rule. Though "the forgiveness of sins" totals but four words in the creed, the truths these words communicate are astounding. These words express the biblical reality of mankind's desperate state before the holy wrath of God against sin. Yet, it also proclaims the incalculable glories of God's grace on the cross of Christ.

In many churches today, there is little declaration of the horror of our sin nor even a confession of sin, which must begin in an acknowledgement of the reality of sin. Evangelical Christianity so often neglects what it means to know, to declare, and to celebrate the forgiveness of sin. Christians remain in a constant danger of following in the footsteps of countless others who have departed from the knowledge of sin and forgiveness. Erroneous teachings abound that seek to diminish the doctrines tied to the Christian belief of the forgiveness of sins.

It is vital for Christians today to understand, grasp, and apply the doctrines tied to this phrase in the Apostles' Creed. A withdrawal from a robust and biblical understanding of the horror of sin necessarily diminishes the beauty, power, and splendor of the gospel of Jesus Christ. Contained in the affirmation "the forgiveness of sins" is nothing less than the heartbeat of all our hope as believers. Christians, therefore, must strive to believe every dimension of this quintessential declaration found in the Apostles' Creed. Failure to glory in the depths of the doctrines that we are about to explore cripples Christian hope, praise, and obedience. Without "the forgiveness of sins," there is no gospel—there is no hope for the people of God, for there will be no people of God.

"Forgive us our sins" is one of the most cherished (and most urgent) pleas found in the Lord's Prayer—the prayer that Jesus taught his disciples to pray. But in order to understand this heartfelt plea to God, we must first understand the reality of our sin. This means the sinfulness of the entire human race, and it also means the horrible reality of our own individual sin.

When we confess that we believe in the forgiveness of sin, we are affirming an entire theology from creation to the fall into sin to God's work of redemption to Christ's eternal kingdom. The entire Christian faith rests in those words—*the forgiveness of sin*.

We now turn to mine the depths of the creed's teaching on the forgiveness of sin. To begin we must recognize the universal plight of all mankind. Next, we must attempt to wrap our minds around the unfathomable revulsion of the nature of our sin. We must try, in other words, to see our sin as God himself does. By understanding our sin aright, the illuminating splendor of the cross of Jesus Christ stands infinitely more beautiful to behold and proclaim. Only through recapturing the universal and horrific state of our sinfulness can we begin to understand the resplendent glories of the gospel and the immeasurable grace of God in forgiving our sin.

For As in Adam All Die—the Total Depravity of Mankind

"In the beginning, God created the heavens and the earth" (Gen. 1:1). The Bible begins with God creating the heavens and the earth out of nothing. He made all things by the power of his Word. The crowning moment of creation culminated with Adam and Eve, divine image bearers commissioned by God to be fruitful, multiply, and fill the earth with more image bearers (Gen. 1:28). This divine drama begins with man living in perfect harmony with God. Indeed, Genesis 1:31 ends with, "And God saw everything that he had made, and behold, it was very good." Very good indeed.

Then, however, comes Genesis 3, when Adam and Eve tore apart the fabric of perfect love and harmony that existed between themselves and God. Adam and Eve disobeyed the command of God. As the biblical text makes evident, they wanted to be *like God*. Their pride plunged the creation into futility. All creation succumbed to the divine penalty of their rebellion. The good world God made now exists under condemnation through the sin of Adam and Eve. This penalty not only came upon the creation, but most importantly, upon all mankind.

As the story of the Bible unfolds, the crushing reality of sin only intensifies. Each subsequent chapter from Genesis 3 on seems only to intensify the curse of the fall. The corruption of sin culminates in the judgment of God in Genesis 6 as God destroys the earth and wipes it clean from the taint of mankind, except for Noah and his family. After the flood, however, the story of sin continues. Mankind cannot escape the curse that began in the garden with a man, a woman, a serpent, forbidden fruit, and a perfect, holy God.

The curse of Adam spread to every corner of creation. This contagion exists in all of us. The Bible teaches in detail the depth of our depravity:

- For all have sinned and fall short of the glory of God. (Rom. 3:23)
- There is no one who does not sin. (1 Kings 8:46)
- No one living is righteous. (Ps. 143:2)
- If we say we have no sin, we deceive ourselves, and the truth is not in us. (1 John 1:8)
- And you were dead in the trespasses and sins in which you once walked, following the course of this world, following the prince of the power of the air, the spirit that is

now at work in the sons of disobedience—among whom we all once lived in the passions of our flesh, carrying out the desires of the body and the mind, and were by nature children of wrath, like the rest of mankind. (Eph. 2:1–3)

- We have all become like one who is unclean, and all our righteous deeds are like a polluted garment. We all fade like a leaf, and our iniquities, like the wind, take us away. (Isa. 64:6)
- Behold, I was brought forth in iniquity, and in sin did my mother conceive me. (Ps. 51:5)

Each of these passages detail the undeniable corruption at the core of every man, woman, and child. In Psalm 51 David noted that even upon his conception, sin was there. No person can reach the standard of God's perfection and holiness. We are born in sin because in Adam we *are* sinners, and we bear the imputation of his guilt. We are born in sin. No human being stands as righteous before a holy God. How can any of us presume to stand before the judgment seat of God as one perfect when we are *dead* in our trespasses and sins?

The result of this crushing indictment upon all mankind consummates the promise of the curse in Genesis 3. The Bible says, "For as in Adam all die" (1 Cor. 15:22). *All* mankind dies in Adam. The totality of this judgment extends to every corner, every pocket, every crevasse of the globe. You and I and all humanity stand condemned before God because of our sin and our union with Adam. As long as man lives under the headship of Adam, he stands condemned. Mankind awaits the execution of eternal judgment and justice as the fury of God will crush sin and all who rebelled against him, his goodness, and his glory.

The Immeasurable Horror of Sin

The belief in the total depravity of mankind that leads to an eternal death should display the unquestionable horror and offense of sin. After Nathan confronted David about his adultery and murder, David wrote these words:

> Have mercy on me, O God,
> according to your steadfast love;
> according to your abundant mercy
> blot out my transgressions.
> Wash me thoroughly from my iniquity,
> and cleanse me from my sin!
> *For I know my transgressions,*
> *and my sin is ever before me.*
> *Against you, you only, have I sinned*
> *and done what is evil in your sight,*
> so that you may be justified in your words
> and blameless in your judgment. (Ps. 51:1–4)

David's sin tormented his very bones. He could not escape from the piercing condemnation of his sin and rebellion against God. He could not get his sin out of his sight. When he turned to the left or the right, his iniquity was there. When he looked up or down, there he found his sins. Even if he shut his eyes, his sins had engraved themselves on the back of his eyelids.

He also grasped the essence of his sins. He understood that his sin was against God and God alone. In 2 Samuel 11 we learn that King David had sinned greatly when he lusted after a woman who was the wife of another man. David increased his sin when he committed adultery with this woman and then sent her husband, Uriah, to die in battle. These gross sins, however, all pale in comparison to where his offense truly lay—he sinned against the eternal Creator, the King of kings, the Lord of lords.

The contemporary culture, however, loathes any such notion of the horror of sin and its consequences. Americans flock to preachers who do not proclaim the reality of sin. Preachers of the prosperity gospel abhor the notion of presenting the true weight of sin for fear of sounding too negative. The gospel they preach—a false gospel—promises prosperity, when our greatest need is not wealth (nor health), but salvation, redemption, *Christ*! Modern Christians, unarmed with the teachings of the Scriptures, often run to the authorities of pragmatic preaching and find moralistic therapy devoid of any biblical truth. Therapeutic deism from talk-show hosts and grinning televangelists has replaced the infallible, inerrant, perfect, and powerful Word of God—and the saving gospel of Jesus Christ.

Christians find themselves in a crisis of truth. A deficient grasp of the horror of sin empties the cross of Christ of its splendor. It is necessary, therefore, to understand the total and universal depravity of all mankind. Christians must go where David did. All must see their sin as God himself sees it.

The failure to grasp the horror of sin rests in the miniature god Christians have fashioned in their own image. Christians are guilty of diminishing the holiness and grandeur of God's incomparable glory. We cannot rightly understand the graveness of our offense if we do not behold the glory of the One we offended. Puritan preacher George Swinnock wrote, "If God be so incomparable, that there is none on earth, none in heaven comparable to him, it may inform us of the great venom and malignity of sin, because it is an injury to so great, so glorious, so incomparable a being."[1] Sin, therefore, must be measured in the depth of its offense against the splendor of the One it offended. If God be so infinitely glorious, more glorious than all the stars of the galaxies combined, then the weight of our sin against this God embodies evil of the highest order. Another Puritan, Jeremiah Burroughs, drew out this implication:

> So strike at God and you wish God would cease to be God. This is a horrible wickedness indeed. . . . What will you say to such a wickedness as this, that it should enter into the heart of any creature, "O that I might have my lust and, rather than I will part with my lust, I would rather God should cease to be God than that I would leave my lust."[2]

Christian, your sin amounts to nothing less than a desire for God to cease being God. Your sin rebels as cosmic treason. Your sin against God beckons him to step off his throne that you might ascend its steps. Your sin wishes the Creator to relinquish his rightful rule and claim to glory and give way to your will.

We fail to grasp the weight of sin because we fashioned a small god to worship rather than the splendid, infinite, supreme, excellent, beautiful, and eternal Creator. We have a shallow view of his glory. Swinnock concluded,

> How horrid then is sin, and . . . heinous a nature, when it offendeth and opposeth not kings, the highest of men, not angels, the highest of creatures, but God, the highest of beings; the incomparable God, to whom kings and angels, yea, the whole creation is less than nothing! We take the size of sin too low, and short, and wrong . . . but to take its full length and proportion, we must consider the wrong it doth to this great, this glorious, this incomparable God.[3]

If Christians are to glory in the riches of the forgiveness of sins, then they must first cast down the inglorious, unholy idols they have fashioned and called "god." Christians must come and behold the terrifying and awesome glory of God in order to grasp the horror of sin. Failure to see God in all his glory necessarily leads to a diminished view of sin. An anemic view of sin will give way to a cheap gospel, a pointless cross, and a Messiah who need not to have shed his blood.

The Danger of an Inadequate Understanding of Sin

An inadequate definition of sin leads to disastrous consequences. Some may think that the view of sin as described above leads to unnecessary feelings of guilt. A temptation arises to dampen such "harsh" teachings on sin in order to proclaim a more uplifting and positive message. For the Christian this must be avoided at all costs. To jettison the horror of sin will lead to a capitulation on essential gospel truths and will insult the cross of Christ. The following are several examples of what happens when Christians fail to recognize the gravity of sin's offense.

Pelagianism. In the fifth century a Roman teacher named Pelagius began teaching against the original sin of mankind. He taught that the nature of man was inherently good and capable of choosing God apart from the grace of God. Pelagianism, therefore, opposes the universal and total depravity of mankind after the fall of Adam and Eve. In other words it opposes the Bible. Falling into the belief of Pelagianism may seem appealing, for it asserts the general goodness of man's nature. Pelagianism seems more optimistic than the notion of original sin and the corruption of man's state. It fails, however, to grasp the weight and horror of Adam's sin in the garden. A belief in Pelagianism not only rejects the Bible's clear teaching on total depravity but leads to a diminished view of our nature, which subsequently draws us away from our sole need of God's grace for salvation.

Roman Catholicism divides sins into two categories, mortal and venial sins. Mortal sins constitute a grave action done with deliberate intent and with full knowledge. Committing a mortal sin places a Catholic on a trajectory for hell unless they repent. Venial sins are lesser sins and by far the most common of sins among Catholic beliefs. A venial sin may meet some of the criteria of a mortal sin but not all its requirements. Venial sins must be confessed for they may lead to mortal sins, but they do not separate a Catholic from grace.

The Bible, however, makes no such distinctions. We must avoid any efforts to reduce the horror of any sin. Every sin breaches the word and command of God. Every sin flows from a corrupt heart longing for God to step off his throne. The Catholic position, furthermore, demerits the unquenchable need for God's grace. Every sin we commit merits the eternal wrath of God. Romans 6:23 says, "For the wages of sin is death." This is the cost of sin. This is the state of all mankind.

Prosperity Gospel. Finally, the prosperity gospel spreads a dangerous, deadly, and eternally disastrous understanding of sin. The prosperity gospel and its teachers do not want to discuss the graveness of sin for they consider it a negative message that detracts from their positive and uplifting messages. By pushing sin into the shadows, "easy believism" permeates prosperity teaching. Prosperity teachers do not present their hearers with the devastating state of their sinfulness. Instead, sinners are often told that they are victims of their circumstances rather than sinners against a holy God. This teaching not only amounts to absurdity but a deadly proclamation. The prosperity gospel merely massages the consciences of its hearers, who are never confronted with their sin, with the righteousness and holiness of God, and with their need for the saving, atoning work of Jesus Christ.

Each of the three categories presents a real danger that detracts from the true teaching of human sin. Christians must fight against such notions and proclaim the truth the Bible presents. All mankind, under the headship of Adam, is dead in sin. Every human stands condemned before a holy and just God. Romans 8:7 says, "For the mind that is set on the flesh is hostile to God, for it does not submit to God's law; indeed, it cannot." Indeed, all apart from Christ are in the flesh. All apart from Christ remain in their sin. This sin is horrific for it is against none other than the high and holy God of the universe. The reality of our sin must be seen in all its horror. Without grasping our need and the gravity of our sin, we will never understand the truly insatiable beauty of what it means for our sins to be forgiven.

Hope Breaks In

All humanity stands condemned before God for the horrific sin that indwells each person. The revulsion of sin cannot be fully comprehended, as we cannot measure the fullness of God's holiness. Man stands, nonetheless, as the perpetrator of the highest treason all the universe has known. We cannot escape this impending doom and judgment of God. We are indeed guilty of all the crimes laid at our feet. What can we do? Nothing. What do we need? Forgiveness. Thus enters the atonement of Jesus Christ, bursting into the cosmic courtroom. This is where hope breaks in like bolts of lightning across the night sky.

The atonement of Jesus Christ on the cross becomes the only hope for all humanity. Hebrews 9:24–26 displays the glory of this hope:

> For Christ has entered, not into holy places made with hands, which are copies of the true things, but into heaven itself, now to appear in the presence of God on our behalf. Nor was it to offer himself repeatedly, as the high priest enters the holy places every year with blood not his own, for then he would have had to suffer repeatedly since the foundation of the world. But as it is, he has appeared once for all *at the end of the ages to put away sin by the sacrifice of himself.*

Once again, we confess the saving truth that Christ is our Great High Priest, who was himself the sufficient sacrifice for our sins. When we confess together that we believe in the forgiveness of sins, we agree with the Scriptures as we are told that Jesus came to save sinners (1 Tim. 1:15); though "while we were still sinners, Christ died for us" (Rom. 5:8) and that, as John reminded us: "For God so loved the world, that he gave his only Son, that whoever believes in him should not perish but have eternal life" (John 3:16). The gift of eternal life is made possible because of the forgiveness of sins—a forgiveness that is only possible because Jesus Christ died for our sins.

Hebrews 9 enshrines the atonement of Jesus Christ as the event all history waited for. The entire creation groaned for that day when Christ would hang on the tree in place of sinners. The promise of God in Genesis 3 to crush the head of the serpent was fulfilled in Christ's work. All the drops of blood shed in the Old Testament sacrifices were but mere shadows longing for the day when the once-for-all sacrifice would be made. All the sins of

God's people were placed upon Jesus Christ. God poured out the fullness of his wrath upon his Son. *How can this be?* We have seen the incalculable horror of our sin. We know the extent of our depravity. We know that we are dead. We know that we followed Satan. We know our hearts longed for God to exist no longer. Despite all our sin and the graveness of the offense, there is Jesus Christ, paying its price.

There is Jesus, on the cross that we deserved for all eternity, bearing the punishment for our sins. As Paul wrote, "For our sake he made him to be sin who knew no sin, so that in him we might become the righteousness of God" (2 Cor. 5:21). What an astounding truth! Hope breaks through the chronicles of humanity's sinful history as God's Son ascends the sinners' hill to bear the wrath reserved for *our* sin. He bore our sins, and we are given the full forgiveness of sins. This is the earth-shaking truth at the center of the Christian faith.

The glories of the atonement encapsulate the constant Christian responsibility to safeguard and teach a robust doctrine of sin. The church must preach the reality and horror of sin. The church must proclaim the universal and total depravity of all mankind. If preachers empty these teachings from the pulpit, they empty the power and glory of the atonement from their messages. Unless sinners see the reality of their sin, they will not look to nor grasp the saving power of the atonement of Jesus Christ.

Hope Accomplished

The atonement of Christ enables and secures the confession of the Apostles' Creed, "I believe in the forgiveness of sins." We have seen, however, the unquestionable weight of what it means for our sins to stand forgiven. The offense was more than our minds could bear, yet Christ bore its punishment fully. He experienced every part of the wrath of God for us. His atonement paid the full price of our sins and bestowed upon us his righteousness.

Understanding the reality of the atonement leads us now to the hope accomplished. "If we confess our sins, he is faithful and just to forgive us our sins and to cleanse us from all unrighteousness" (1 John 1:9). This verse bears the fullness of Christian hope. Sinners can confess their sins to God. Why? Because Christ paid the price in his body on the tree. He became the curse for us. We can confess our sins and be confident of forgiveness because Jesus bore the penalty. Though our sin be great and its offense too vile to look upon, Jesus paid its debt. Though the wages of sin is death, God accomplished the free gift of eternal life through Jesus' sacrifice.

Christians who fail to understand the true notion of sin deny themselves the only hope they have in Jesus Christ. False teachings on sin will inevitably lead to a works righteousness, a cheap gospel, and a Christ senselessly murdered. God's plan of redemption through Christ need not have happened if sin is easily conquerable by human initiative. The dread of sin and its consequences leads all to the need for God's grace through the gospel of Jesus Christ. This is the great paradox of the Christian life. The world longs for us to run away from our guilt. Guilt is seen as an enemy that must be killed. Self-help books fill the shelves of bookstores as people ruthlessly try to squash the inner feeling of guilt. For the Christian, however, guilt is a gift. That feeling of unquenchable, unyielding guilt, leads us to the only hope we have. Sinners must embrace the infinite guilt they live in if they are to find the infinite grace of God. As we embrace our guilt, then and only then can we come to that crimson fount of hope, the blood of Jesus that washes us clean.

In 1 John 1:8–9 we find the promise that undergirds our belief in the forgiveness of sins: "If we say we have no sin, we deceive ourselves, and the truth is not in us. If we confess our sins, he is faithful and just to forgive us our sins and to cleanse us from all unrighteousness." Note the assurance of this promise. If we confess our sins, he is faithful and just to forgive our sins. We are called to confess our sins, individually and corporately— continually. God forgives us our sins, and because of the atonement perfectly and constantly accomplished by Christ, he is faithful and just to do so. Faithful, because God always keeps his promises. Just, because, as the old gospel hymn reminds us:

> Jesus paid it all,
> All to Him I owe;
> Sin had left a crimson stain,
> He washed it white as snow.[4]

Conclusion

The Apostles' Creed, in a few short words, proclaims the infinite glory of the Christian gospel. The incomparable horror of sin is wiped away through the forgiveness of God bought by Christ's atoning work. The creed's candor on the true state of humanity reveals that we are a people in need of eternal forgiveness. Contained within the words "I believe in the forgiveness of sins" is nothing less than the everlasting hope of all mankind. To believe in the forgiveness of sins means that we know who we are apart from Christ. We must realize the vile nature of our sin.

We must recognize our helpless state as those dead in Adam. Contained, too, in the affirmation of the forgiveness of sins is the accomplishment of Christ's work. We need not nor dare not add anything to the creed's affirmation. To do so would be tantamount to preaching a false gospel.

The danger, however, resides in the temptation to abandon all that this affirmation teaches. To teach the total depravity of man seems too harsh and pessimistic of humanity. To proclaim the horror of each and every sin seems too harsh in a world trying to escape from the feeling of guilt. To preach a need for forgiveness assaults human pride that longs to prove itself before a holy God. Each of these temptations must be killed with every word of the Bible and gospel truth. We must not depart from the affirmation of the Apostles' Creed. To do so would be to rob ourselves, our churches, and the world of the only hope of all mankind—the precious atonement of Jesus Christ through his bloody sacrifice that washed us clean. It is through his blood—and his blood alone—that we can be washed as white as snow. This is the gospel.

CHAPTER FOURTEEN

THE RESURRECTION OF THE BODY AND THE LIFE EVERLASTING

I can remember, as a child, hearing people talk about heaven and being worried that it was like sitting in a pew for eternity. I loved coming to church, but I couldn't imagine sitting any longer than I had to sit. My mind was tempted to wander in so many different directions as my feet were dangling over the pew, unable to even touch the floor. I can remember hearing about heaven and being unable to imagine it. Indeed, Christians can actually *not look forward to heaven*, especially if we think unbiblically of heaven, which many Christians do. Our unbiblical conceptions of the eternity to come betray us.

Christians have staked our lives on the eschatological hope of the resurrection of the body and the life everlasting. The Christian life is marked by a yearning for that eschatological hope. The apostle Paul wrote, "For the creation waits with *eager longing* for the revealing of the sons of God" (Rom. 8:19). Since the fall of Adam and Eve, death entered the world, resulting in the entire creation desperately longing for redemption. Paul continued:

> For the creation was subjected to futility, not willingly, but because of him who subjected it, in hope that the creation itself will be set free from its bondage to corruption and obtain the freedom of the glory of the children of God. For we know that the whole creation has been groaning together in the pains of childbirth until now. And not only the creation, but we ourselves, who have the firstfruits of the Spirit, groan inwardly as we wait eagerly for adoption as sons, the redemption of our bodies. (Rom. 8:20–23)

Though we know that Christ paid the price for our sin and crushed the head of the serpent, death still exists. Christians and the entire cosmos eagerly await and yearn for that final victory over Satan and death. Therefore, to be Christian is to yearn. To be a follower of Christ means yearning for that day— the redemption of the *body*.

This eager yearning for the final redemption of our bodies brings us to the final section of the Apostles' Creed:

> I believe in the Holy Spirit,
> in the holy catholic Church,
> in the communion of saints,

the forgiveness of sins,
the resurrection of the body,
and the life everlasting.

This summary statement of the Christian faith points to the end for which each believer in Jesus Christ eagerly awaits. These final words encapsulate the glories of the age to come. This creed ends not with a whimper but with a bang! It declares the truth of what we believe as Christians about the end of time: the resurrection of our bodies and the life everlasting. If the Christian life yearns for this promised, eternal state, however, we need to ask, "What is the resurrection of the body? What is the life everlasting?" Sadly, a deficient view on these glorious truths impoverishes the faith of too many Christians. As a result, many believers do not live with the confident expectation for the future that the Bible teaches, and this produces a detrimental consequence on life and ministry in the present. Recapturing the Bible's instruction on the resurrection and the life to come becomes an absolute necessity so that the glories of these promises to come might enrich our present yearning and deepen our longing for that day when we will no longer walk by faith but by sight.

The Resurrection of the Body

A Christian Understanding of Death

The Apostles' Creed ends assuming its readers understand what happens between the forgiveness of sins and the life everlasting. We must not forget, however, that the decay and death of the body comes in between our forgiveness and our resurrection. The Bible describes death as the final enemy. This means Christians look upon death in at least two ways. First, we look at death in a dreadful way. Fear in the sense that death leads to an end of earthly life, of something precious. Second, and more important, Christians see death as an enemy and the object of our hatred. The final destruction of death will thus be the destruction of our great enemy. The Lord's Day will come and the final victory shall be won. On that day, the dead shall rise! This resurrection from the dead will not be a mass resuscitation. It is a *resurrection*.

From Death to Resurrection—an Exposition of 1 Corinthians 15

In the doctrine of the resurrection, far too many Christians fail to rest and to exult in the riches the Bible presents. First Corinthians 15 displays the eternal promise of the resurrection of the body and its centrality to the Christian hope.

"Most to Be Pitied?"

1 Corinthians 15 beautifully displays the glory of the gospel. In the context of 1 Corinthians 15, however, Paul's main concern does not first center on the denial of *the resurrection of Christ* but on the denial of *the resurrection of the body*. This explains Paul's logic in 1 Corinthians 15:12–20:

> Now if Christ is proclaimed as raised from the dead, how can some of you say that there is no resurrection of the dead? But if there is no resurrection of the dead, then not even Christ has been raised. And if Christ has not been raised, then our preaching is in vain and your faith is in vain. We are even found to be misrepresenting God, because we testified about

God that he raised Christ, whom he did not raise if it is true
that the dead are not raised. For if the dead are not raised,
not even Christ has been raised. And if Christ has not been
raised, your faith is futile and you are still in your sins. Then
those also who have fallen asleep in Christ have perished. If
in Christ we have hope in this life only, we are of all people
most to be pitied.

But in fact Christ has been raised from the dead, the firstfruits of those who have fallen asleep.

Paul centralized the hope of all Christians in the resurrection
of Jesus Christ. Without the resurrection of Jesus, the Christian
faith is a vain faith. It misrepresents God and his will. Indeed,
without the resurrection of the body, Paul said Christians still
live in their sins. Yet Christ *did* rise from the grave! He paid
the price of our sins. He now sits enthroned over the cosmos.
Christians then are not a pitiable people. In raising Christ from
the dead, God made him the firstfruits. As he was raised bodily
from the grave, so Christ's people will also be raised from death
to eternal life. Jesus lives, even now, as the tangible evidence of
God's promise for the resurrection of the body for his people.

Yearning for the End

After showing the hope Christians have of their own resurrection in the resurrection of Christ, Paul moved on to show us *how*
this happens.

For as by a man came death, by a man has come also the resurrection of the dead. For as in Adam all die, so also in Christ
shall all be made alive. But each in his own order: Christ the
firstfruits, then at his coming those who belong to Christ.

Then comes the end, when he delivers the kingdom to God the Father after destroying every rule and every authority and power. For he must reign until he has put all his enemies under his feet. (1 Cor. 15:24–25)

In this text Paul argued the stark differences between Adam and Christ, or death and life. Paul explained that by Adam, death entered the world; through Adam, condemnation came to all mankind. Paul made this point clear:

Therefore, just as sin came into the world through one man, and death through sin, and so death spread to all men because all sinned . . . For if many died *through one man's trespass* . . . Because of *one man's trespass*, death reigned through *that one man*. (Rom. 5:12, 15, 17)

Thus, central to Paul's theology is the headship of Adam for all mankind. Through Adam death and sin spread to all men. Our position in Adam enslaved us to death and Satan. With Adam the head of humanity, mankind lies helpless and inextricably linked to the judgment and wrath of God.

Yet, in Christ, God offers a new federal head who brings freedom and hope to all who look to him in faith. The condemnation of the headship in Adam in Romans 5 now reverses. Jesus Christ and his righteousness lead to justification and life for all who look on him (v. 18). Through Jesus' obedience many will be made righteous (v. 19). All the inheritance of Adam's headship passes away as new life in Christ solidifies a new and lasting inheritance of life everlasting. With Christ comes the resurrection from the dead (1 Cor. 15:21). In Christ all will be made alive (v. 22).

First Corinthians 15 displays the drama of the consummation of the ages. The hope of the resurrection and eternal life embodies what Christians yearn for at the day of Christ's appearing. Thus, the glory of Christian yearning lies in the object of our yearning; that is, we yearn for that which will not fade, for something that will never pass away, for a life of eternal joy and peace in Christ. Paul illustrated the depth of this yearning: "Then comes the end, when he delivers the kingdom to God the Father after destroying every rule and every authority and power. For he must reign until he has put all his enemies under his feet" (vv. 24–25). At the coming of Christ, the end comes. Christ will overthrow every demonic rule and satanic authority. All the nations will crumble before him. Every enemy of his will succumb to his infinite power and unquestionable authority. All his enemies, including Satan and death, will be destroyed and put under his feet. Christ inaugurates a new kingdom where death is defeated and Satan cast away for all eternity. The final triumph of Christ over his enemies and his eternal reign comprises the incomparable end for which Christians hope and long.

A Peculiar Glory

Paul's theology only deepens as he expounds even more glorious truths surrounding the resurrection of the saints. In the verses that follow, Paul specifically details the nature of the resurrected body. He details a peculiar glory that believers will realize on the Day of Jesus Christ.

But someone will ask, "How are the dead raised? With what kind of body do they come?" You foolish person! What you sow does not come to life unless it dies. And what you sow is not the body that is to be, but a bare kernel, perhaps of wheat or of some other grain. But God gives it a body as he has chosen, and to each kind of seed its own body. For not all flesh is the same, but there is one kind for humans, another for animals, another for birds, and another for fish. There are heavenly bodies and earthly bodies, but the glory of the heavenly is of one kind, and the glory of the earthly is of another. There is one glory of the sun, and another glory of the moon, and another glory of the stars; for star differs from star in glory.

So is it with the resurrection of the dead. What is sown is perishable; what is raised is imperishable. (1 Cor. 15:35–42)

Because of sin, nothing in a person merits an immortal hope. Yet, by God's grace and love, by his sovereign power, the physical body perishes, yet God will raise it to life. Though the pangs of death still loom on the horizon, Christians live in an absolute confidence that what was sown in dishonor will be raised in honor. What was sown in weakness will be raised in power. What was sown as perishable will be raised as an imperishable body.

Yet what will this imperishable body look like? What attributes come with this new body? First, the resurrected body is a physical body. This may go without saying, but this must be explicitly affirmed. The physical body is part of what it means to be human. Christians, therefore, will have a corporeal, physical, bodily existence throughout eternity. Thus, a resurrected, glorious, physical body will have some continuity with the bodies we have now. There will be, however, stark discontinuity between the old perishable bodies and the new eternal bodies. What was weak will give way to power. What was dishonorable will give way to honor. What was natural will be transformed to spiritual. What was perishable will give way to an imperishable body that will never see or taste death.

These bodies will live in immortality with Christ for all eternity. First John 3:2 exclaims, "Beloved, we are God's children now, and what we will be has not yet appeared; but we know that when he appears we shall be like him, because we shall see him as he is." When Christ appears, Christians will live with him in a physical existence, in a physical body. Yet this body will shine in glorious perfection for all eternity, seeing and savoring Christ face-to-face forever.

Oh Death, Where Is Your Victory?

In the final verses of 1 Corinthians 15, Paul began to write of a mystery. This mystery that Paul unfolded in these verses bring to a climax his teaching on the resurrection and its implications. Though what he tells us is indeed a mystery, by God's grace through regeneration, we can grasp what Paul detailed in these final verses:

> I tell you this, brothers: flesh and blood cannot inherit the kingdom of God, nor does the perishable inherit the imperishable. Behold! I tell you a mystery. We shall not all sleep, but we shall all be changed, in a moment, in the twinkling of an eye, at the last trumpet. For the trumpet will sound, and the dead will be raised imperishable, and we shall be changed. For this perishable body must put on the imperishable, and this mortal body must put on immortality. When the perishable puts on the imperishable, and the mortal puts on immortality, then shall come to pass the saying that is written:
>
> > "Death is swallowed up in victory."
> > "O death, where is your victory?
> > O death, where is your sting?"

> The sting of death is sin, and the power of sin is the law. But thanks be to God, who gives us the victory through our Lord Jesus Christ.
>
> Therefore, my beloved brothers, be steadfast, immovable, always abounding in the work of the Lord, knowing that in the Lord your labor is not in vain. (1 Cor. 15:50–58)

In this passage Paul told the Corinthians that when the day of the Lord comes, some who have not yet tasted death will transform into their new, glorious bodies. Thus, at the second coming of Christ, whether alive on the earth or six feet under, all those who are united to Christ by faith will undergo a glorious transformation.

Why must Christians undergo this transformation? Because, as Paul tells us, *perishable* must put on *imperishable*, and *mortality* must put on *immortality*. In that moment death, which lingers as the creation's and the Christian's final enemy, will be swallowed up. On that day of resurrection and transformation, the death of death finally occurs. The saints and all creation will cry out, "Death! Where is your victory? Death! Where is your sting?" The power of sin over all creation will be crushed to oblivion for all eternity, and the victory of Christ will inaugurate the new ages for God and his people. This transformation from mortal to immortal signifies to the universe that God has wrought the final victory of Satan, sin, and death. When Christians put on the new body, they put on the new age of an eternity without death.

"Thanks Be to God, Who Gives Us the Victory Through Our Lord Jesus Christ."

And on the basis of this, Paul wrote, we can then live. Christians can defy death in the sense that they can die safely. In light of that truth, Paul concluded, "Therefore, my beloved brothers, be steadfast, immovable, always abounding in the work of the Lord, knowing that in the Lord your labor is not in vain" (1 Cor. 15:58). Indeed, the labor is not in vain. Christians now see that this life presents grand and glorious opportunities to sow to that day to come. Christians now march to a cadence of victory in the face of death, for they know how this redemptive story will conclude.

Without knowing the culminating event of the final resurrection, Christians cannot function in ministry. If Christians fail to recognize the end for which God destines them, then ministry in the midst of sin, trials, and persecution will be impossible. Indeed, Paul said earlier that if the resurrection is not true, then we are of all people most to be pitied. Why? Because the Christian life is a life of the cross. It constitutes a life of pouring out, laying down, fighting sin, bearing burdens. The Christian meets a hostile, sinful world under the power of Satan. Not only that, the Christian, even after a long and arduous life, must still face that final enemy, death. If then the resurrection and the hope to come exist as a mere fantasy, then all the suffering Christians endure only merits pity of the highest order.

Yet this is not the truth, for the resurrection of Christ *did* happen. He *secured* our hope by his resurrection. The Spirit rests on us as a sign and a seal that indeed we, too, will be raised with Christ. Paul said that the same Spirit that raised Jesus from the dead lives in us and will give life even to our mortal bodies (Rom. 8). Christians then can endure suffering. Christians can face with boldness the harshest persecution. Christians can stare down death knowing that it, too, shall pass when Christ returns. The reality of the resurrection of our bodies frees Christians from all fear and emboldens them to lives of godly zeal. As Christians know where all history will culminate, they can gladly lay their lives down and be that grain of wheat that falls to the ground and dies and bears much fruit. Thus, Christians must yearn for that day of the resurrection. Without yearning for that glorious day, hardness of heart will set in and the fear of death will freeze the affections that should burn with holy passion. In order to live for that resurrection to come, Christians must yearn for it.

The Life Everlasting

The last phrase of the Apostles' Creed adds to what has already been affirmed. The church has exercised great wisdom in distinctively setting apart the "resurrection from the dead" and the "life everlasting." The latter flows from the former, and both come together, postulating one glorious truth of the end times. Thus, "I believe in the life everlasting" affirms that all the dead shall be raised as well as reminds that there is a future judgment.

Earlier in this book, we looked at the reality that Christ will come to "judge the quick and the dead." The life everlasting denotes that the final judgment has arrived. Christ, upon his final victory, will indeed judge all mankind. Jesus made it clear that he will separate the "goats" from the "sheep" (Matt. 25:31–46). On that day he will say something very different to the sheep and the goats. He will essentially say to the sheep, "Come with me into my heaven." He will say to the goats in effect, "Go into a hell of everlasting torment." The judgment of Christ initiates a dual eternal destiny. All will inherit eternal life. Yet those who placed their faith in Christ will enter an eternal life of rest and joy. Those who did not come to the Savior will spend an eternity in the torment of hell. Both realities carry with them eternal sentences. It is vital that Christians read this creed as detailing both the joys of heaven and the dread of hell. *Both* are coming in that day of Christ.

Though eternal death awaits those who do not place their faith in Christ, for Christians eternal life in heaven with God stands as their inheritance. The home for Christians will be heaven for all eternity. Yet, so often, Christians fail to yearn for the fulfillment of this glorious promise that Christ secured through his death, burial, and resurrection. Christians are too often satisfied with the world and all its temporal pleasures, forgetting Paul's words:

> If then you have been raised with Christ, seek the things that are above, where Christ is, seated at the right hand of God. Set your minds on things that are above, not on things that are on earth. For you have died, and your life is hidden with Christ in God. When Christ who is your life appears, then you also will appear with him in glory. (Col. 3:1–4)

In this passage, Paul reminds Christians of their identity as those united by faith to Jesus Christ. In light of that identity, Christians must live on this earth as heavenly minded people. Paul commissioned us to seek the things that are above and to seek none other than the risen Christ, seated on his throne. Paul wrote that we have died to this world and that our lives now reside intimately with God. Paul concluded by telling Christians that when Christ returns, we will appear with him in glory forever. Thus, eschatology provides a chief foundation for the Christian life and ethic. As Christians understand the beauty of the inheritance that awaits them, they will then live differently on this earth. Heavenly minded Christians yearn for the eternity to come and live for that eschatological promise made in Colossians 3.

The deficiency of contemporary Christian yearning should cause deep concern. Christians, especially in the West with all its conveniences and wealth, have let the world delude our senses. Christians think that heaven will be something less exhilarating than what we know in this life. Worldly comfort, riches, and fulfillment have clouded Christians' vision of what God made them for, saved them for, and is working all history toward.

Heaven is not a place of less; it is a place of infinitely *more*. All the good things known in this life will either be amplified infinitely in the life everlasting, or they will be transcended by things that are infinitely better. God reveals in his Word the stunning reality of the life to come:

- "In my Father's house are many rooms. If it were not so, would I have told you that I go to prepare a place for you?" (John 14:2)
- "He will wipe away every tear from their eyes, and death shall be no more, neither shall there be mourning, nor crying, nor pain anymore, for the former things have passed away." (Rev. 21:4)
- "But, as it is written, 'What no eye has seen, nor ear heard, nor the heart of man imagined, what God has prepared for those who love him.'" (1 Cor. 2:9)
- "For here we have no lasting city, but we seek the city that is to come." (Heb. 13:14)
- "The wall was built of jasper, while the city was pure gold, like clear glass." (Rev. 21:18)

That last verse was the foundation of Jonathan Edwards's sermon, "Nothing Upon Earth Can Represent the Glories of Heaven." Edwards resolved that even the language of the Bible

cannot fully describe the joy to come, for the Bible must condescend to our fallen and limited perceptions. Edwards concluded
his sermon,

> It appears [Christians] shall be thus exceeding blessed and
> glorious, because they shall enjoy God as their own portion,
> and shall fully enjoy the possession of all things. The infinite
> God gives himself to them to be enjoyed as much as to the
> full of their capacity. Certainly, therefore, the doctrine must
> be true, that nothing earthly can give us a representation of
> their glory; so certainly silver, nor gold, nor precious stones,
> nor crowns, nor kingdoms can be in any measure compared to
> the infinite God. Besides, they shall also with him possess all
> things fully. Because they shall see God's face, and enjoy God
> as his own dear children.[1]

Edwards called the Christian to rightly contemplate the glories of heaven to come. The loftiest of human language cannot
contain the riches awaiting the saints. Heaven comprises the
highest of all joys, the deepest of all pleasures, the highest wonders the universe will ever know; and it will be the occupation of
the Christian to take it all in and glory in it forever!

Yet, I see so little yearning for that day. Christians must
awake from their slumber and shake off the numbing pleasures
of this world. This world will never satisfy. Indeed, Edwards's
final words in that famous sermon state,

> How unreasonable are they who grudge to deny themselves
> for the sake of heaven. Truly no rhetoric can represent their
> folly. How great folly must it [be] for men to shrink at mor-
> tification and self-denial for a few days for such a degree of

happiness as this who can't care to deny the cravings of an appetite or their slothfulness for such manner of glory.[2]

Such glory awaits all those who trust in Christ. Will Christians, even in the comfort of Western civilization, cast off the vestiges of a world passing away and *yearn* for a glory that surpasses all understanding? How sad it is, as Edwards exclaimed, that many will forsake the weight of infinite glory and joy for a few fleeting moments of pleasure in this life.

That is why the Christian life cannot be understood apart from yearning. Christians must be a people who yearn for the resurrection to come when death and Satan are finally defeated. Christians must yearn for the resplendent glories of being in the presence of the Trinity for all eternity, knowing that even after ten thousand centuries of unexplainable felicity, they will not have shaved off one second of their time in heaven. Only through this yearning can the Christian endure persecution, mortify the flesh, wage war against Satan, and press on for the prize of the resurrection of the body and the life everlasting.

Final Words

Sometimes, the Apostles' Creed survives even in the worship of churches that have otherwise abandoned the faith. Its historic stature means that some liberal churches continue to recite the Apostles' Creed despite the fact that they have adopted a liberal theology that is incompatible with the creed. They dare not remove it. Their own congregations would revolt.

So there it is, recited every Lord's Day, and not without effect.

When a pastor friend heard that I was writing this book, he eagerly told me of his own upbringing in a liberal Protestant church. There was no theology, no doctrine, and no Bible from the pulpit. The worship was largely empty of content, except for historic hymns and the recitation of the Apostles' Creed.

My friend told me that as a teenager reciting the creed in worship, even in the midst of a theological desert, he realized that this creed *is* Christianity—that the Christian faith is a truth claim and that the truths affirmed in the creed are *true*. "The Apostles' Creed was the only link to biblical Christianity I ever heard as a teenager," he told me. He held onto the words of the creed with all his might.

Christians through the centuries have confessed the faith of Jesus Christ—the faith Jesus taught his disciples, the faith the apostles taught the early church, the faith "once for all delivered to the saints" (Jude 3). The Apostles' Creed is just one treasured summary of the Christian faith, but it is the most commonly confessed doctrinal statement in Christian history. Martyrs have confessed this creed. It is named for the apostles because the creed can be traced back to the faith and doctrines the apostles received from Christ and taught to the church. It was honored by the Reformers and is found in and behind virtually every orthodox statement of Christian belief.

The Apostles' Creed does not exhaust the Christian faith—no summary can. But Christians through the ages have declared it boldly—even in the face of dictators, even in the face of death. When we confess this faith, we take up our place in the long line of Christian faithfulness that is now more than two thousand years old. I marvel at the privilege, and I am astounded by the boldness of a confession that begins with God the Father Almighty and concludes with life everlasting. Between the beginning and the end of the Apostles' Creed is the entire body of biblical truth with the gospel of Jesus Christ as its center.

This is the faith of the Christian church. This is the faith of the people of God. This is the faith of those purchased by the blood of Christ. This is the faith once for all given to Christ's church.

Have you ever thought of the Apostles' Creed as a prayer? In its own way it is. And, like a prayer, it ends boldly.

The Apostles' Creed ends with one word: *amen*. We agree, amen. As the entire world knows what we believe, amen. As the church exalts in Christ, amen. As we believe, teach, and confess the faith that Christians throughout the ages past have confessed and will confess for infinite years to come: amen, and amen.

ACKNOWLEDGMENTS

Once again, it is time to express gratitude in print. No project like this emerges from a vacuum or without countless kindnesses and assistance. The Christian life is one long (even eternal) exercise in gratitude. This is the right time to pause and say thanks to many who helped along the way as I was writing and working on this book.

My life at Southern Seminary depends upon the outstanding work of so many, including the staff of the Office of the President. Jon Austin, chief of staff and assembler of the team, begins the list. Among his many gifts is the power of encouragement. Sam Emadi was my director of research when the project began, and Cory Higdon took over as the project came to a close. I am deeply in debt to both, scholars in their own right. Interns in my office included Mitchell Holley, David Lee, Ryan Loague, Ryan Modisette, Bruno Sanchez, and Troy Solava. They are all keen readers and great conversationalists. Jonathan Swan, another brilliant young scholar, served as my librarian and was constantly able to find books when I could not.

I am very thankful for Colby Adams, communications

director for my office, who also serves as producer for *The Briefing*. The excellent team at Thomas Nelson is headed by Webster Younce, who knows books as few people know books. I deeply appreciate him and the publishing and editorial team he leads. Once again, I have depended upon representation by Wolgemuth and Associates, and I am thankful for the friendship and faithful advice of Robert Wolgemuth through the years and for the excellent work of Andrew Wolgemuth on this project and so many others.

One of the great joys of my life is working with the outstanding Christian scholars who are the faculty of The Southern Baptist Theological Seminary and Boyce College. Individually and together they make a massive contribution to the lives of students, and to my life as well. I am thankful for the support of a wonderful board of trustees. Every day I am reminded of the privilege of working with three incredible senior vice presidents, Randy Stinson, Matthew Hall, and Craig Parker.

My family has been wonderful, as always. My mom, Janet Mohler, is always a source of encouragement. Though she now loves us through the horrible fog of Alzheimer's disease, she loves us always, and we love her even more. She can no longer read my books, but I write them for her nonetheless. I love you, Mom.

Our son Christopher keeps me humble, making me laugh at myself. Our daughter Katie Barnes and her husband Riley Barnes just make us unbelievably happy, and that happiness and love are only multiplied beyond calculation by our grandsons, Benjamin and Henry. Time seems to stop when they are with us, and nothing but love can explain it.

And, speaking of what only love can explain—how could I even know who I am without the constant love and joy of my wife, Mary? There is no part of my life that she does not enliven, enrich, and encourage. After thirty-five years of marriage, our lives are so interwoven that I cannot imagine any project, any book, any sermon, any task, any day without her. Saying thank you to Mary is hardly adequate, but it is a good place to start and, for this statement of gratitude, the right place to end.

Soli Deo Gloria

NOTES

Introduction

1. Jaroslav Pelikan, *The Emergence of the Catholic Tradition* (Chicago: Chicago University Press, 1971), 1.
2. Jaroslav Pelikan, *The Vindication of Tradition* (New Haven: Yale University Press, 1986), 63.

Chapter 1: God, the Father Almighty

1. Gordon D. Kaufman, *God the Problem* (Cambridge, MA: Harvard University Press, 1972).
2. A. W. Tozer, *The Knowledge of the Holy* (New York: Harper One, 1961), 1.
3. Carl F. H. Henry, *The God Who Speaks and Shows*, Vol. 3 of *God, Revelation, and Authority* (Wheaton: Crossway, 1999), 405.
4. John Calvin, *Calvin: Institutes of the Christian Religion*, ed. John T. McNeill, trans. Ford Lewis Battles, 2 vols. (Philadelphia: Westminster, 1960), 1:108.
5. N. Abercrombien, "Superstition and Religion: The God of the Gaps," *A Sociological Yearbook of Religion in Britain* (London: SCM Press, 1970), 93–129.
6. Helmut Thielicke, *The Waiting Father: Sermons on the Parables of Jesus* (Cambridge: Lutherworth Press, 2015).

7. Mary Daly, *Beyond God the Father: Toward a Philosophy of Women's Liberation* (Boston: Beacon Press, 1973), 19.

8. Carl F. H. Henry, *God, Revelation and Authority* (Illinois: Crossway, 1999), 5:159.

9. 217th General Assembly Council, "The Trinity: God's Love Overflowing," 2006.

10. 217th General Assembly Council, 398–99.

11. 217th General Assembly Council, 420–21.

12. 217th General Assembly Council, 423–24.

13. 217th General Assembly Council, 408–9.

14. Pietro Martire Vermigli, *The Peter Martyr Reader*, ed. John Patrick Donnelly (Kirksville, MO: Truman State University Press, 1999), 9.

Chapter 2: Maker of Heaven and Earth

1. Langdon Gilkey, *Maker of Heaven and Earth: A Study of the Christian Doctrine of Creation* (Garden City, NY: Doubleday, 1959). Langdon Gilkey recognized that the doctrine of creation stands at the very center of Christian theology. As he further makes clear, "If this is not the God who is Father of the Lord Jesus Christ, the biblical story makes no sense whatsoever."

2. Gilkey, 18

3. William Blake, *Songs of Innocence and of Experience* (London, 1874), 89–90.

4. Blake, 53.

Chapter 3: Jesus Christ, His Only Son, Our Lord

1. George Tyrrell, *Christianity at the Cross-roads* (London: Longmans, Green and Co., 1913), 44.

2. Stephanie Innes, "'Lord' Is Fading at Some Churches," *Arizona Daily Star*, April 22, 2007, http://tucson.com/lifestyles/faith -and-values/lord-is-fading-at-some-churches/article_edff2a01 -0a35-53b4-bd28-c740f81a28ff.html.

Chapter 4: Conceived of the Holy Spirit . . .

1. Irenaeus, *Against Heresies*, 5.1.2–3.

2. Augustine of Hippo, *Sermons to the People: Advent, Christmas, New Year, Epiphany,* trans. William Griffin (New York: Crown Publishing Group, 2002), 55–56.

3. Adolf von Harnack, *The Acts of the Apostles,* trans. J. R. Wilkinson (London: Williams & Norgate, 1909), 298.

4. Wayne Grudem, *Systematic Theology: An Introduction to Biblical Doctrine* (Grand Rapids: Zondervan, 1994), 530.

5. Peter Martyr Virmigli, *Early Writings: Creed, Scripture, Church* trans. Mario Di Gangi and Joseph C. McLelland, The Peter Martyr Library 1 (Kirksville, MO: Thomas Jefferson University Press, 1994), 37.

6. Carl F. H. Henry, "Our Lord's Virgin Birth," *Christianity Today,* December 7, 1959, 20.

7. Donald Macleod, *The Person of Christ* (Downers Grove, IL: IVP Academic, 1998), 37.

Chapter 5: Suffered Under Pontius Pilate

1. Isaac Watts, "When I Survey the Wondrous Cross." Public domain. This was taken from *Hymns and the Faith* by Erik Routley, printed in Greenwich, Connecticut in 1956.

Chapter 6: Was Crucified, Dead, and Buried

1. John Stott, *The Cross of Christ,* anniv. ed. (Downers Grove, IL: IVP Books, 2006), 131.

2. Peter Taylor Forsyth, *The Cruciality of the Cross* (London: Hodder & Stoughton, 1909), 44–45.

Chapter 8: The Third Day He Arose Again from the Dead

1. John Calvin, *Institutes of the Christian Religion,* Book 2, Chapter 16.13, page 521.

2. Grudem, *Systematic Theology,* 828 (see chap. 4, n. 4).

Chapter 9: He Ascended into Heaven and Sits at the Right Hand of God

1. Grudem, *Systematic Theology,* 841 (see chap. 4, n. 4).

2. Grudem, 620.

Chapter 10: Whence He Shall Come to Judge the Quick and the Dead

1. N. T. Wright, *Surprised by Hope: Rethinking Heaven, the Resurrection, and the Mission of the Church* (New York: HarperOne, 2008), 180–85.
2. Anthony Hoekema, *The Bible and the Future* (Grand Rapids: Eerdmans, 1979), 253–54.

Chapter 12: The Holy Catholic Church and the Communion of Saints

1. D. A. Carson, "Evangelicals, Ecumenism, and the Church," in Kantzer and Henry, *Evangelical Affirmations*, eds. Kenneth S. Kantzer and Carl F. H. Henry (Grand Rapids: Zondervan, 1990), 366.

Chapter 13: The Forgiveness of Sins

1. George Swinnock, *The Works of George Swinnock, M.A.*, vol. 4 (Edinburgh, Scotland: Banner of Truth Trust, 1992), 456.
2. Jeremiah Burroughs, *The Evil of Evils: The Exceeding Sinfulness of Sin* (Morgan, PA: Soli Deo Gloria Publications, 1992), 40.
3. Swinnock, *The Works of George Swinnock*, 456.
4. "Jesus Paid It All," *HymnWiki*, last modified April 24, 2010, https://www.hymnwiki.org/Jesus_Paid_It_All.

Chapter 14: The Resurrection of the Body and the Life Everlasting

1. Jonathan Edwards, et al., *The Works of Jonathan Edwards*, vol. 14: *Sermons and Discourses: 1723–1729* (New Haven: Yale University Press, 1997), 154.
2. Edwards et al., 159–60.

ABOUT THE AUTHOR

R. Albert Mohler Jr. is president of the Southern Baptist Theological Seminary and the Joseph Emerson Brown Professor of Christian Theology. Considered a leader among American evangelicals by *Time* and *Christianity Today* magazines, Dr. Mohler can be heard on *The Briefing*, a daily podcast that analyzes news and events from a Christian worldview. He also writes a popular commentary on moral, cultural, and theological issues at albertmohler.com. He and his family live in Louisville, Kentucky.